Writer Wellness works...

"I was impressed with the idea of using wellness techniques to help with writer's block. From my perspective, I could see how a person could carry over those same techniques and skills to other aspects of their life. Writer Wellness *is very thought provoking and presents a realistic and pragmatic means to improving one's self."*

— Debbie Lazorik, Athletics Director,
Marietta College

"Finally, a reference book for writers that focuses on the physical well-being of the writer, not the prose."

— Aleta Dodson, President,
Central Ohio Fiction Writers

"As an educator, one of the most difficult fundamentals to instruct is how to give students the tools with which to be creative. Ms Held offers both practical skills and sound advice that take any level of writer from beginning steps to total wellness."

— Brian Palmer, Professor of Dance,
Jacksonville University

"Writer Wellness is theoretically sound, eminently practical, and presented in a format that makes the reader feel like a participant in an engaging workshop on creativity. This book should deflate the notion that good writing emanates from dissipation rather than in spite of it."

— David L. Keller, Professor of Humanities,
Ohio Valley College

"Not only does Ms. Held supply a roadmap to discovering inner creativity, she paves the road as well!"

— Phyllis Jean Adams, *Romantic Times* Convention Newsletter Editor

Writer Wellness

A Writer's Path to Health and Creativity

By

Joy E. Held

New Leaf ✧ Illinois

Medical disclaimer: Participation in the exercises and diet contained in this book is done at your own risk. The suggestions in this book are not intended to replace the recommendations of your health care practitioner. Consult a physician before engaging in any change of diet or exercise program.

A New Leaf Book
Published by WigWam Publishing Co.
P.O. Box 6992
Villa Park, IL 60181
http://www.newleafbooks.net

Library of Congress Catalogue Card Number: 2003106225
ISBN: 1-930076-00-2

Photography by Jody Purkey

Printed in the U.S.A.

Dedication

My love and thanks to Sandy, Sherrell, Wilma, and Bonnie for participating in Writer Wellness Workshop when it was just an idea and for sharing their worlds and words with me.

My unconditional love to Aurora, Kitri, and Christopher forever.

Acknowledgements

These people always supported me in or out of the box: my family, Teresa Basile, Joan Berolatti, Charis Calhoon, K.C. Patrick, Cathy Roedersheimer, Tony Tokarz, and Mary Young.

Table of Contents

Introduction

This book is about the rest of your life. If you choose to follow any of the suggestions given, you will become aware of the myriad of changes the human body, mind, and spirit experience on any given day in any given lifetime. And that's good for you as a writer, because writing is many things, but most importantly it's the permanent expression of your unique interpretation of the world.

Your vision, your point of view, is valuable whether it agrees with others or not. You have the right to contribute to the destiny of the human species with your take on the world. Awareness is integral to your ability to define life. So you need a life to define.

In the delivery room, the first of sign of life is movement. The lack of movement is also the first sign of death in a being. The healthy integration of physical movement with mental powers is the best sign that we are alive. Studies abound declaring the mind-body connection, and appreciation of what role the spirit plays in being human is expanding as well.

Our awareness as writers depends on our state of health physically, mentally, emotionally, and spiritually. Our choices have a profound effect on the condition of these factors. It's better to make decisions that lead to a healthy state of being that is supportive of a creative way of life. The information in this book presents choices you can make to improve yourself by writing in a journal, exercising regularly, learning to relax or meditate, making sound nutritional decisions and by engaging in some creative "play." Everything has been tested on writers and artists in other fields such as dance and visual arts. Participants noticed a positive change in their health and increased ability to accomplish their creative desires.

In every main concept chapter there is a list of Writer Wellness Cornerstones that recap the important information. Read the chapter, review the Cornerstones, then continue on to the exercises meant to clarify particular points with hands-on activities.

The main idea chapters have a special section at the end entitled, Creative-While-You-Work, with suggestions for incorporating the exercises into your workday. This should help ingrain the ideas and guide you to a new life as a healthy writer.

The simplest way to use this book is to devote daily reading time to small sections, perhaps at night before going to bed. Have a pen handy while you read to make notes in the margins. Digest the material before attempting the exercises. Plan to spend ten to fifteen minutes a day on the exercises and move on anytime you feel compelled. Also, skip exercises if you want and return to them later.

The quality of time is more important than the quantity of time. Choose fifteen-minute periods that are most likely to be free of interruptions. Read, exercise, journal or complete an exercise when you're ready. Every reading or exercise section is virtually self-contained, but the entire process is interdependent. While some pieces will benefit you, the complete package will change your life and your writing.

Besides this book, the tools and toys necessary include:

* Writing and drawing tools (pens, pencils, crayons, etc.)

* A blank journal

* A calendar with large blank squares

* Art supplies (glue, scissors, construction paper, etc.)

* Old magazines

* Walking shoes/exercise clothing
* Relaxation kit (candles, lavender oil, pillows, etc.)
* 3 X 5 note cards
* A blank notebook for the exercises and your personal notes
* A timer (watch, electronic timer, etc.)

Some of you will read through the whole book and catch the exercises later. That will work as long as you stay dedicated to the process in small increments. Assess your life and set aside whatever time blocks you have that will allow you to reap long-term benefits of the overall concept. Basically, this means gently and gradually restructuring your writing, fitness, relaxation, nutrition and creativity until you have permanent changes that will sustain your career.

A popular writing exercise in many creativity and writing classes has students write their own obituary or epitaph noting everything they would like to have accomplished with their lives. The morbidity of this idea is stifling, but students are asked to somehow get beyond visualizing their own deaths and construct a plan for what and how they really want to be remembered as writers. This plan is supposed to guide them to authentic writing that doesn't waste anyone's time.

"Shock-education" is similar to "scare-parenting" where you take a three-year-old to the street to point out a dead rodent and say, "That's what you'll look like if you don't stay out of the street." The obit exercise is useful to the beginning journalism student whose first job on the daily newspaper will probably be collecting and writing funeral announcements, but a reporter is rarely asked to write their own and never left in this job for too long. While the obit exercise gets a student's attention, it doesn't promote positive change.

Life-affirming exercises produce the best results. The following is such a powerful and essential tool, it's the first exercise in this book:

"I believe."

Write these words at the top of a clean sheet of journal paper. Pause and reflect for a moment. Something you believe will come to mind. Write it down. Then continue to write the words "I believe, I believe, I believe" as many times as you have to until ideas jump out at you. Write them down, each time beginning with the words "I believe." Don't edit, revise or filter anything. Write what comes to mind. After at least two pages of beliefs, reread your work. Make a concluding statement and put the exercise away. You should do this once a month in your journals.

An intense truth begins to expand itself the more you practice "I believe" writing. Some of your beliefs will cause you to stop and think. Other themes will repeat themselves month after month. These are your gut components showing themselves so you can connect with them in your life and in your writing. It's a much happier way to discover your truths and desires than contemplating how people will remember you by writing your own epitaph. Swear a pact with yourself to make the choices now that will imprint your beliefs on the world and your world will never forget you.

Writer Wellness

WHAT IS WRITER WELLNESS? More than seven years ago, I ran into an emotional wall that threatened to dismantle my writing career.

I was a successful freelancer published in trade journals, regional newspapers and poetic circles. After many years of deadlines and editors who didn't return phone calls, I chose to set aside bylines for raising and home-educating two wonderful daughters. My intention was to return to writing when they were old enough to open the "canned pasta with red sauce" unassisted. Eleven years later, the day arrived when my oldest daughter made lunch for herself and her sister without my help. I headed for the computer.

I tried to write; I read self-help titles, and I tried to attend a critique group, but no amount of external action seemed to get me back on track. I finally listened to my soul and heard her say, "You have all the answers within."

A trite cliché, you say, but years as a dancer, actress and teacher had taught me that listening is the fundamental basis of all the arts. I listened.

Talking to myself was nothing new. I had recorded my life's internal conversations in a diary since the age of eight, but that, too, had fallen by the wayside and been replaced by nurturing others. The beloved cartridge pen and trusty spiral notebooks called to my inner sister—the one who runs around barefoot in flannel pajamas yelling, "Listen! Will you listen to yourself?" I returned to journal writing.

Each time I spent twenty or thirty minutes writing down my feelings, thoughts and daily drudge, I noticed a cleansing breeze rush through my body and mind like a spiritual enema. I cleared my head of daily "stuff" and was amazingly able to sit in stillness again and write poetry and articles without teeth gnashing. Within months, I was gifted with a dream that served as the foundation for my first romance novel.

Besides writing ever since I can remember, the other half of me has spent almost every afternoon of forty odd years in our family dancing school. My mother has operated the school, riding the waves of whatever movement fad comes along, for over fifty years. Even falling off a stage at the age of sixty-six and almost bleeding to death from the severed artery didn't stop her from teaching her ballet classes. By example, she has shown me that good exercise and nutrition, with some dogged persistence thrown in, can save your life.

Along with the freedom to write creative works, I sensed a change in my maturing body. Ballet class four times a week hurt like hell at age thirty-six. I quit, or was thrown out, (I haven't resolved that yet) and returned to yoga. Yoga had been one of those "fads" my mother had me ride for her. When the local YWCA called in 1977 and asked if we had anybody who could teach yoga, my mother said, "Of course." She handed me a book and said, "Read this. You are teaching a class of twelve women in two weeks." I read the book, showed up in my leotard and gave a class. The next week there were twenty-four women in the class. I was eighteen years old and it was ego-building until I learned how much I earned compared to what the YWCA kept. After the class ended, I taught in other places where my cut was more respectable. It's never been much, but it's better today than 70/30 (me on the slim side). But yoga isn't about money.

I loved yoga and incorporated its principles of peaceful stretching into all the dance I taught for years to come: ballet, belly dancing, ballroom dance, aerobic dance, line dancing, tap, jazz, (you get the picture). No one ever got injured in my classes because I taught deep breathing with long slow postures no matter what the genre.

Back to being thrown out of ballet class. Three years later I was leading writing workshops, teaching yoga, and finishing my novel. The regimen of daily journal writing, exercise, relaxation and proper nutrition easily fell into place for me because of my background. I finally finished a historical romance tome of which I was really proud, volunteered for local and state writers' groups, and published poetry and articles anywhere I submitted. Other writers began to ask my advice about their work and about getting over personal hurdles they felt were keeping them from being satisfied as creative artists.

When I thought it over, I had followed my own program for more than three years and the results were exciting. I felt better and wrote better and more easily than ever before. The teacher, mother and writer in me recognized a way to help others. The result was Writer Wellness Workshop.

I've been teaching Writer Wellness Workshop for over seven years now, and practicing what I preach for more than ten years. The program has led many a writer out of the depths of creative hell to the wide open fields of artistic freedom. You can go there, too.

WRITER WELLNESS CORNERSTONES

* Listening is the fundamental basis of all the arts.
* You have all the answers within yourself.

What Is Writer Wellness?
Exercises
(* use a timer)

JOURNAL

List everything and everybody, large and small, that is "in your way" to realizing a creative dream. Don't hold back. Purge your system of every detail that you feel has, does, or will impede your creative progress. Just vent. (* 5 minutes)

EXERCISE

Walk away from your house, apartment, or workplace for exactly two and a half minutes. At that point, turn around and walk home. Any pace will do, but build up to a brisk jaunt. (* 5 minutes)

RELAX

Lie down on your back on a bed. (Take off your shoes!) Cover your eyes with an herbal eye pillow or a warm folded washcloth. (To warm a cloth, open and sprinkle water on the center, fold over and microwave for 20-30 SECONDS. Check the heat intensity on the inside of your arm before placing the cloth over tender eye area.)

Be as physically still as possible. Breathe normally through the nostrils and count fifty breaths (one inhale/exhale is one breath). Lie still for the remainder of the time if there is any. (* 5 minutes)

NUTRITION

Buy and eat one of the following foods that you've never tried before.

Wheat-free cookies	Rice crackers	Egg substitute
Spelt bread	Rice milk	Nondairy cheese
Spelt pasta		

CREATE

Presenting Me Poster. Buy a large sheet of poster board. Use any medium (paint, markers, stickers, etc.) to entitle the poster "Presenting Me..." writing in your name after "Me." Place the title anywhere you want on the poster.

Spend up to ten minutes a day over the course of a week collecting and affixing items, ideas, pictures and statements that identify your image of you as you see yourself. Examples: poetry or quotes you like or have written, photographs with you in most of them, your favorite things (my poster includes a white sock glued on because I love wearing sparkling white, cotton socks), magazine images that depict some aspect of your personality, names and pictures of family members, pictures depicting your dreams and goals.

One student drew a picture of her published novel but covered it with a lift-up flap of computer printout paper from her job. She said it symbolized how work kept her from attaining her goal.

CREATIVE-WHILE-YOU-WORK IDEAS

Take "Presenting Me" into work if you can and display it at your workstation for a few days. If the poster is too big to take with you, create a scaled down version by taking a photograph of the finished poster and displaying the picture at work. Or perhaps you can add dimension to the study by creating a smaller version on construction paper. Repeat as many themes as you like from the original poster and add anything spontaneous that occurs.

Close the door on your office, lunchroom or closet and practice the five-minute relaxation exercise described above every day for a week. If you can't find a door to close for privacy, simply sit up straight in your office chair with feet squarely on the floor. Close your eyes and rest both hands on your thighs, palms up. According to many yoga practices, upward facing palms is a position of receptivity and peacefulness. Practice the deep breath relaxation for at least five minutes. Display a "Resting! Back in five minutes" sign on your desk if you have to!

Before eating lunch, walk away and back to work five minutes as described above.

Take your sandwich to work made with spelt* bread instead of white or wheat.

* Spelt is a grain that is suggested for persons who need to avoid wheat products. It's available at many health food stores.

Why Wellness Is an Important Investment

Healthful living is not a new idea. Ancient civilizations revered the fit and vigorous person for their physical condition, cosmetic beauty and longevity. Healthy people live longer. Leonardo da Vinci recorded his rules for health in the fifteenth century:

"To keep in health these rules are wise:

* Beware of anger and avoid grievous moods.

* Rest your head and keep your mind cheerful.

* Be covered well at night.

* Exercise moderately.

* Shun wantonness, and pay attention to diet.

* Eat only when you want and sup light.

* Keep upright when you rise from the dining table.

* Do not be with the belly upwards or the head lowered.

* Let your wine be mixed with water, take a little at a time, not between meals and not on an empty stomach.

* Eat simple (i.e., vegetarian) food.

* Chew well.

* Go to the toilet regularly!"

(From *How To Think Like Leonardo da Vinci. Seven Steps To Genius Every Day* by Michael J. Gelb.)

The wellness lifestyle enables you to live a longer, more vital and productive time on earth.

Specifically, Writer Wellness is regular journal writing, exercise three to six times a week, daily relaxation and/or meditation, proper nutrition including dietary supplements, and creative play on a regular basis. There is a host of additional ideas to incorporate into your writing life to sustain your creativity and your health like aromatherapy, travel, and music, to name a few. Like most wellness programs, Writer Wellness is lifestyle adjustments you can live with forever. The *forever* keeps it from being a fad.

WRITER WELLNESS CORNERSTONES

* Healthful living concepts date back many centuries.

* Healthy people live longer and enjoy life more.

* Writer Wellness is regular journal writing, exercise, daily relaxation or meditation, proper nutrition and creativity.

Why Wellness Is An Important Investment Exercises
(* set a timer)

JOURNAL

Copy into your journal one of Leonardo da Vinci's "rules for health" as listed in this chapter. Respond in your own words how you can implement this rule into your life. (* 5 minutes)

EXERCISE

Twisting Breath

Stand (or sit up straight in a hard chair, not on a sofa) with your feet hip distance apart, toes pointing straight ahead.

Inhale and raise your hands to your chest, palms facing the floor, fingertips touching, elbows held out to the sides.

Exhale and twist to one side as far as you can from the waist, (try to face the back of the room). Inhale and return to the front. Exhale and twist to the other side. A twist right and then left equals one set. Complete ten sets. Rest. (* 5 minutes)

RELAX

Play soft, relaxing music and rest on your back with your eyes closed for five minutes. Use an eye pillow or warm cloth across your eyes to increase the efficiency and intensity of this restorative session.

As you relax, focus on your breath and "watch" it enter and leave your body. (* 5 minutes)

NUTRITION

At a restaurant or at home, eat all fruit and vegetables for one meal. Caution: breading contains wheat flour. This is not a vegetable. Eat a hearty meal of a raw salad, several different cooked vegetables (up to four different kinds) for the main entrée, and fruit salad or gelatin with fruit for dessert. Drink one or more large glasses of water with this meal.

CREATE

List the three most important goals in your life. Choose a color that symbolizes that goal for you. For example:

"Finish novel"=purple

"Learn to meditate"=yellow

"Write a new poem"=green

Cut the appropriately colored construction paper into fun shapes large enough to write your goals on. You need five shapes for every goal, fifteen in all (i.e., five purple, five yellow, and five green). Write the date on the back of each shape.

Write your goal on the fronts and post the goal shapes in places you frequent: the bedroom, bathroom, kitchen, office, car, your wallet, etc. Leave the shapes in place no matter how ragged they get until you achieve the goal. Take them down, write the finish date on the back and celebrate in your journal.

CREATIVE-WHILE-YOU-WORK IDEAS

Write da Vinci's rules for health on individual 3 X 5 note cards. Take a different rule to work with you each day in your wallet or purse. Take the card out and read it at least once during the day. Try to think about the rule several times a day.

Practice ten sets of Twisting Breath every day before eating lunch. This will take approximately one and a half minutes.

Take your important goals shape cards to work and post them in places on your desk, door or in a drawer that will help keep them on your mind throughout the day.

What Is a Creative Writer?

A better question is, What is the difference between a *creative* writer and an *uncreative* writer?

To answer this question, I first have to accept that there is such a thing as *uncreative*. I don't. In my world, the only way someone can be uncreative is to be completely without effort, someone who doesn't try at all. My definition of creative is so expansive and accepting that I am unable to comprehend uncreative.

But most people, and this might include you, feel that only a chosen few are *creative* and the rest either are or have to learn to be creative. That's the point. The sheer effort it takes to learn (and I use that term very loosely) to be creative is indeed a creative act. This is very much like "Which came first? The chicken or the egg?" I've come to the conclusion that I'm never going to get that one, but I really, truly believe that all people are born creative. You can have the same belief if you give credence to my definition of artistic genius.

When I meet someone, they automatically receive the benefit of the doubt. I trust that they are creative people. They come to me with an automatic one hundred percent on the un-standardized test of inventiveness. I do this because that's the way I want to be treated—with respect for my unrealized creative efforts. They are unrealized because I haven't needed them yet. When I do, they will appear. This is a universal truth. The definition, therefore, has to be rather liberal in order to allow for the unborn ideas of everyone else.

Creative people:

discover
persevere
think deeply
ask questions
use plot webs
get the facts
have multiple perspectives
talk
write
paint
argue
have fun
smile
invent things
are quiet
concentrate
focus
make mistakes
study
look for connections
like new things
tell jokes
love nature
are awed
are emotional
are satisfied
glow differently
have a sense of wonder
recognize effort

analyze
understand
know failure
know success
dig deeper
know flow
are flexible
dream
walk
dance
cry
laugh a lot
use tools differently
observe
listen
are loud
play games
breathe deeply
read
balance
are persistent
are always learning
are nonjudgmental
are respectful
solve problems
use resources
are not satisfied
exercise
respect differences

are thankful
are passionate
act
produce
sculpt
notice details
fear time
sing
direct
play music
see things from a different perspective
don't know that they are creative.

According to Ned Herrmann in his book *The Creative Brain*, "Creative people live as if there were no tomorrow, which is part of what enables them to be passionate about today." Could your degree of passion for life and work be connected to your health and emotions?

Somewhere in this list you can find something to identify with. If you can't, take a pencil and scribble your idea of what it is to be creative on the list, because you are a *creative person.*

WRITER WELLNESS CORNERSTONES

* Creativity has an expansive and unique definition to fit everyone if observed from a liberal perspective.

* All people are born creative and packed with unrealized creative efforts.

What Is A Creative Writer?
Exercises
(* set a timer)

JOURNAL

Copy into your journal all the "creative people definitions" from the list in this chapter that you feel apply to you. Add any ideas of your own. With the time left, explore your feelings about accepting such a wide range of ideas as the definition of a creative person. (* 5 minutes)

EXERCISE

You need an exercise book from the library or one of your own. The more pictures and descriptions of exercises, the better. Choose at least three exercises from the book and adapt them to your physical needs and abilities. Write your variations down in your journal or an exercise journal and give the adaptations new descriptive names, (i.e., "Joy's Just Right Jumping Jacks"). Perform these three custom designed exercises every day for a week. (* 5 minutes)

RELAX

Spread a blanket on the floor and lie down on it. Support your head and neck if you want, and place a rolled pillow under your knees if you have back problems.

Rest your palms on top of your abdomen and breathe normally through your nostrils for five minutes. Notice if your abdomen muscles rise and fall with each breath. Encourage this action if you can.

To stand, roll over to one side and use your hands to push up to sitting. Wait a few moments before standing. (* 5 minutes)

NUTRITION

Choose one meal today that you can take a long time to eat. Don't read while eating, but easy listening music in the background is acceptable. Calm nature sounds are the most soothing while eating.

Think about the details of how the food arrived at your table and everything involved in getting it into your body: the growing, harvesting, shipping, selling, preparing, chewing, swallowing, etc. Make a concentrated effort to appreciate every bite of the entire meal. Write about this experience in your journal.

CREATE

Gather five recyclable/reusable items like plastic bottles, egg cartons, toilet paper tubes and an old toothbrush. Anything will do. Next, you need a strong background like foam board or cardboard to create a collage with the recyclables and any other art or craft supplies you have (paints, markers, crayons, etc.).

Use all five pieces in the same collage if you can. For example, draw or paint a scene with a monster and use the head of the toothbrush for his hair or teeth. Glue on a piece of the egg carton to create his space ship. Cut the toilet paper tube in half length-wise and decorate it for the monster's body. You get the "picture." See these throw-aways as adaptable to representing something from your imagination.

CREATIVE-WHILE-YOU-WORK IDEAS

Take one day and jot down a brief list of some of the things you do at work. Set aside a piece of paper, index card or small notebook and simply stop every so often during the workday and make brief notes of what you've done. At the end of the day, review your list and write one of the items from the creative list above beside every activity. For example:

Drove to work via reroute around bad traffic-"solve problems"

Did chair exercises at break-"exercise"

Fixed copier with letter opener-"use tools differently"

The possibilities are endless. The idea is to recognize your life as creative achievement from sun up to sun down.

"I'm Busy Enough"

But are you making the most of your creative energies? The Writer Wellness lifestyle is the simplest and best use of your time outside of writing because it channels the excess brain and body sludge that invariably gets in the way of creativity.

For example, if you are dragging around some emotional baggage about an argument you've had with someone, chances are really good that you will be distracted by worry and frustration while you're writing. If a scene in your novel calls for a hot disagreement between your characters, then you might be able to use up your own irritability on your story. This doesn't always work.

It's better to have a daily sit down with your journal and a pen and pound out both sides of the argument for the satisfaction of seeing yourself right in print. Even a five-minute journal session helps immensely. Draining your emotional garbage in this way frees up your creative juices to flow in harmony with your ideas.

Without developing this process you risk falling prey to a marketing ruse known as "writer's block." Sorry, but that's another creativity myth. The term "writer's block" is way overused and invoked way too many times as a justifiable reason not to write. It's better to admit to yourself and others that you just aren't writing. That's all. Just not writing right now. There's no shame in not writing for the public. You will write later. Later when you've cleared your mind, body and spirit of the daily build up of gobbledygook collected from normal life. Everyone has it.

As a writer, you can't afford for it to clutter up your mind or your pages. It creates wordiness and generally unintelligible jargon that gets you into trouble with editors.

Get it out of your brain by journal writing every day. Get it out of your body by exercising every day. Get it out of your spirit by meditating or relaxing every day. Get the nausea out of your belly by eating better so you won't be brought down by the normal emotions of everyday living and you will never, ever suffer from "writer's block" again. When you aren't writing, you simply aren't writing for the eyes of the public. You are writing in your journal for your eyes only. And that's a very worthwhile and creative effort.

WRITER WELLNESS CORNERSTONES

* Daily mental and emotional drudge is best dumped into a personal journal rather than into a creative project.

* "Writer's block" doesn't really exist.

* The creative process is better served if the mind, body and spirit of the artist are cleansed on a daily basis with journal writing, exercise, relaxation/meditation and proper nutrition.

"I'm Busy Enough" Exercises (* set a timer)

JOURNAL

The Music Man (the Broadway musical) claimed, "Ya got trouble!"

Life isn't perfect. Everyone's got a trouble or two.

Draw a circle in the center of a journal page. Write your trouble in this bubble. Draw four spokes radiating north, south, east and west from this "trouble bubble." Attach a "solution bubble" to the end of each radius.

In each "solution bubble," write or draw any idea (no matter how ridiculous or fantastical) that could solve the problem. Add "solution bubbles" until your trouble is clearly outnumbered by all the potential ways to end it.

Choose one possible solution and write a paragraph about how it could work to solve your problem. (* 10 minutes)

EXERCISE

Break a sweat. Dress warmly, include a hat. Take a brisk, five-minute walk away from the house. Turn and walk home even faster if you can.

When you return, stretch your calves out with the runner's stretch: Facing the wall, put both hands on a wall and walk backwards about two feet. Place one leg further behind you, pressing the heel to the ground while bending the other knee. Hold for twenty seconds. Stretch the other leg.

Take a cool shower. (* 15 minutes)

RELAX

Lie on the floor on your back. Support your head or neck if necessary. Start at your feet with a tense-relax scan of your body.

Lift the right leg slightly off the floor. Inhale and tense your leg. Exhale and lower the leg. Repeat in succession for your left leg, hips, right arm, left arm, upper back and face.

Finally, inhale, tense and lift your whole body by digging heels, fists and the back of your head into the floor simultaneously. Exhale and lower your body. Notice the draining sensation as tension leaves your body. Lie still for five minutes. (* 15 minutes)

NUTRITION

One morning, spend an extra ten minutes preparing and pre-packing all fresh, raw vegetables for snacks. Wash, cut and bag three to four pieces of carrots, broccoli, cauliflower, celery, green pepper, zucchini or summer squash to be eaten every time you have the munchies. Make five to six snack bags. Eat small amounts several times that day and drink plenty of water.

CREATE

Design some "Emotional Baggage." Take a shoebox and tape the lid on to one side so that it opens like a piece of luggage. Decorate the outside however you like, but somewhere print "Emotional Baggage. Handle With Intention To Lose."

Fill the "suitcase" with concrete representations of your emotional hang-ups, troubles, dilemmas, sticky situations and general difficulties. Anything you worry about or obsess over should be in this box.

Write the troublemakers on note cards, slips of paper or fancy shapes you've cut out. Further represent them with magazine pictures, plastic figurines or just about anything that lends a concrete visual to the problem.

Feel free to add worries anytime, but be prepared for your troubles to disappear after creating this exercise. When they dissolve, remember to remove the symbol from your "Emotional Baggage" and celebrate.

CREATIVE-WHILE-YOU-WORK IDEAS

Use the "trouble bubble" exercise to solve a problem at work.

Do five minutes of light exercise before lunch and five minutes of relaxation after lunch.

Prepare the fresh vegetable snack bags the night before and pack two or three for lunch and breaks at work. Drink plenty of water with raw vegetables.

JOURNAL

How Do I Journal?

What is the best way to journal? If there were just one way, there'd be just one person in the world. So the answer is a multiple choice: a. my way, b. your way, c. by a prescribed format, d. any way at all, e. all of the above.

First, there are some basic truths about your journal writing that you absolutely must accept. Write them in the front of every journal you collect until you know them to be part of your belief system. Here they are:

1. "This is my truth at this moment." What you write in your journal is your truth at the moment you write it. That truth, while circling your fundamental beliefs, is flexible and changeable. This is positively acceptable because your journal must be the one place you can explore what your truths are until you develop firm belief foundations.

2. "I accept my journal process as the right one for me." Whatever format, device or ritual you develop that *keeps you writing* in your journal is the right one for you at that time in your life. Stay flexible, however, to changes in your life that also signal that it's time to change your journal keeping process. This is growth and change for the good of your personal progress. Be kind to yourself and expect the changes to occur, especially if journal writing becomes a habitual part of your life.

3. "Whatever time I have to devote to journal keeping is enough." While there are minimums you

should adopt, be responsive and accepting of the time slots you find in the schedule that allow regular journal writing time. You must make a commitment to journal regularly. The time will expand as you and your processes do.

4. "My expectations for this journal will be made known to me as I write." Always avoid predicting, planning or prescribing expected outcomes for your journal writing. The simplest anticipations always net the grandest results.

Let's further explore these concepts as methods for starting, maintaining, and revering your journal writing.

WRITER WELLNESS CORNERSTONES

* This is my truth at this moment.

* I accept my journal process as the right one for me.

* Whatever time I have to devote to journal keeping is enough.

* My expectations for this journal will be made known to me as I write.

How Do I Journal?
Exercises

JOURNAL

Write the "journal basic truths" in the front cover of your current journal. Write them again every day as the first part of your daily journal entry for one week. Follow each day with whatever else is on your mind. Use the truths as something to write about when you feel stymied on a topic or can't think of anything to write or can't face what your heart wants you to write down.

EXERCISE

Walking at any pace is the most basic exercise routine there is. Walk for up to twenty minutes a day for a week and journal about how you feel physically and mentally. Better or worse? (If you have a physical disability that prohibits freedom to walk, resort to exercise equipment or basic stretching.)

RELAX

Basic relaxation is stillness of body and mind. Lie down with your eyes closed or covered by an eye pillow for ten minutes a day for one week. Attempt to do this at the same time each day. Strive to be as still as possible except for breathing.

NUTRITION

Research and start taking a basic multivitamin everyday.

CREATE

Buy or borrow a child's coloring book. Get a box of crayons in the eight basic colors. Color a picture every evening for a week. Paste them into your journal.

CREATIVE-WHILE-YOU-WORK IDEAS

Choose a friend or colleague with e-mail capabilities. Spend five minutes every workday sending him/her one short note about your thoughts for the day. Tell your friend not to reply to the e-mails but to print and save them for you. Collect your daily journal briefs at the end of each week to satisfy the journal-writing task. Or you could send the e-mails to your home account and collect them in a journal file. Write longer entries by hand on the weekends and create a journal worthy of any writer.

"This is My Truth at This Moment"

If you've ever planted a garden or some flowers in a pot, you probably checked on the progress of the plants almost every day. And you noticed change when it occurred, and you applauded change as good and symbolic of growth. In the beginning, when the seeds were still and deep in the moist, warm earth, you weren't really sure anything was happening. You just hoped. Your gut told you that even though you couldn't see the changes and growth, it was there, it was happening in spite of the fact that circumstances and situations might not have been perfect. Not enough water because you were gone for the weekend, too much sun because you were late getting home from work and didn't move the pot. Instinctively you *knew* that the changes were occurring. It's the same with your body.

Writing in your journal is the same as planting the seed beneath the dirt and hoping. It takes time to fully recognize the benefits of journaling. You just have to start a journal (plant the seeds), nurture the process by writing daily (provide water and sunlight), and apply faith that something will grow and you'll learn from it (learn to recognize a seedling).

"Every day is a new beginning." Haven't you heard that? Have you maybe heard it enough? The truth can be boring if it doesn't change day after day. But this truth says that your body changes daily and that each day is a chance to start anew. Why? Because there is not one damn thing you can do to change the past. Nothing. The best rule to adopt in your journal is to complain, praise or wonder about yesterday, but don't expect to change it. *Use* it to learn about how you can live today. The best way to use yesterday to your advantage is to record it and learn from it. But today is where you apply those lessons. Just today. Just now. Just this moment. That's all.

So, as your body changes, regenerates, sloughs off and generally does its thing over and over, your spirit and mind probably go through a similar process. This isn't a biology lesson. It's a spiritual one. It's a lesson on accepting things as they are at the moment and learning to write about that and nothing more. "This is my truth at this moment," means finding the stillness inside your brain to really listen to the truth as your body and soul know it at that moment.

Here are some journaling ideas for tapping into your momentary truths:

1. Keep your journal and pen in a secure place beside the bed. Sit up in the morning and write the first thing that is in your mind at the top of a fresh page in the journal. Go about the morning business you absolutely have to, but return to your journal as soon as possible. Develop the idea by writing out a conversation with yourself or an imaginary person about the idea at the top of the page. Be really honest with your writing. Continue to write the first thing that pops into your head until a flow happens.

2. Use relaxation techniques such as deep breathing or meditation before writing. Come to the page as empty and as relaxed as possible. Don't force, but listen intently to what your mind is saying to you, to what your body is telling you, and follow those leads again with the most honest writing you can find within yourself.

3. Play soft instrumental music and listen for about twenty minutes before you sit down to write. Keep the music playing and explore what you hear. Most importantly, don't stop your hand from writing whatever you hear, however you hear it. This is your truth singing through the veil. The best way to meet it is to relax and allow it to control your writing hand for a few lines. Then give another part of yourself the chance to respond. Follow this with more listening, writing and responding until you feel a peaceful ending.

4. Choose a new or different spot to journal. Write a sensory entry about all the sights, sounds, smells, tastes and feelings you encounter. This is good exercise for a coffee shop or park.

WRITER WELLNESS CORNERSTONES

* Change is symbolic of growth.

* It takes time and patience to fully realize the benefits of journal writing.

* Don't try to change the past; learn from it.

* Accept things as they are at the moment and learn to write about that and nothing more.

"I Accept My Journal Process as the Right One for Me"

Your journal process includes all the equipment, tools, ideas, devices and formats you choose to support your progress.

In yoga, I know students are bored when they fall asleep during the relaxation or visualization part of the class. The mind shuts down when it gets bored and some people are literally put to sleep by boredom. Yes, some of them snore. This is a sure sign that they didn't talk to themselves in a gentle, persistent manner to provide the brain with a guided descent into stillness.

Avoid boredom in your exercise and writing program by maintaining a sense of balance between the mindless chatter that goes on in your head and the easy, soothing, conscious response of your relaxation-craved side.

When I was young, my mother told me that boredom was a sign of ignorance. Anybody with a brain who could think had no excuse for being bored. In her world, boredom didn't exist. In a harsh sense, which is how she taught me most of life's important lessons, she was right. As long as I can converse with myself internally, I don't stand a chance of being bored. The only drawback to this method is that I remain perpetually busy physically trying to keep up with all the mental business I generate. I become over-extended in a scheduling sense if I don't monitor myself carefully. Regular journal writing is how I monitor myself.

And then there are the people who prefer to be bored and without responsibilities or challenge. Okay.

When my young daughters expressed this condition, I typed up a two-page, single-spaced list of "Things To Do When You Get

Bored" (See Appendix A, page 160) all chosen to be self-directed and challenging on all levels. They got mad at me. They wanted ME to alleviate their boredom. My mother didn't do it for me. I'm not doing it for my daughters because it's a disservice to the basic human instinct to be creative. I would be interfering with the expansion of their individual artistic growth if I plattered everything up for them to taste. If I did all the work from idea to presentation and then gave them the option to "try it," I would be taking away the essence of what it means to be a creative person: ingenuity.

Developing your journal writing processes is about staying one step ahead of your mind's ability to become bored and fall asleep by assessing what you have to work with, what you want to accomplish, and how you're going to proceed. Keep it linear. Make it easy on yourself to demonstrate positive progress so that you have plenty to celebrate on a steady basis. Celebration is essential to life, creativity, and to writing.

Here are some ideas for accepting your journal process as the right one for *you*:

1. Take some time to answer the following questions about yourself. It's important to write them down on any kind of paper using a pen or pencil. Later you can journal on a keyboard if that's what you decide, but discovering your preferences is better accomplished by sending the answers from your heart, to your brain and through your hand onto paper.

    a. Are you safe or dangerous? Which did you like better as a child: running helter-skelter on the playground feeling the wind in your face, dodging other kids, or a challenging game of kickball run by the rules of the physical education teacher's handbook? Explore what you liked and disliked about each style of play as you answer.

b. Are you brave or timid about learning new skills? Do you prefer fast-moving large groups or detailed, intimate workshops that cater to your individuality? If you have trouble with this question, rethink it and write out how you would teach someone a new skill. Would you choose "monkey-see-monkey-do-follow-the-leader," lecture and reading for knowledge, discovery or something else?

c. What types of entertainment do you enjoy most? What do you dislike about some popular forms of entertainment like reading a book, going to the movies or sports events? Explore your history with these and how they might relate to your choices of entertainment today.

2. Assess finances then visit several stores with varying price ranges that sell school, art, craft, and office supplies. Take the time to handle all the papers, notebooks, writing utensils, stickers, rubber stamps, ribbon, lamps, candles, incense, markers, paints, and ready-made journals available. Make lists of what you like by noticing your emotional satisfactions with each different object. Buy what you like and take it home. You don't have to use all of it right away.

3. Use large sheets of plain paper to write out your typical schedule for a week. Do this by keeping track as you go on a daily basis; write as you live it, in other words. Be detailed. Don't worry about straight lines.

Review your weekly schedule circling the times you could stop doing something like watching television and replace it with journal time. Choose more than one time per day every day and write in potential journal times.

Pre-write the following week's schedule on large blank sheets of paper. Write in the prospective journaling periods, leaving out excess television, phone conversations and anything you can delegate to someone else. Follow this schedule like a dedicated monk for the entire week, even if schedules aren't your favorite thing. It's just one week, not a lifetime.

Note in your journal the times you like best and worst for writing. Make a chart "Journal Time Choices" of the best time slots in your life for productive, undisturbed journal time. You should strive for more than one choice time a day and journal at any of those good periods. It doesn't have to be the same one every day, day after day.

Remember to stay flexible and keep your journaling tools handy but secure so you can write at the best times for you.

WRITER WELLNESS CORNERSTONES

* Boredom is avoided through a sense of balance.
* To be creative is a basic human instinct.
* Keep your journal writing process simple and linear.
* Celebration is essential to life.

"Whatever Time I Have Is Enough"

After discovering what time slots exist in your schedule that allow you to journal, accepting those slots as enough is paramount to success. By success I mean consistency in your devotion to regular journaling and honesty with your words.

The honesty issue is achieved by securing your journal in places that only you can access. Locks, keys, safes, under the mattress, in boxes, locked drawers, beneath your socks in the bureau, wherever you feel safe about leaving the words. Some people have situations that require them to keep their journals with them at all times. I hope your security set up is better than this. With your journal always in a protected location, you can feel more open about writing your truth as you uncover it in your daily entries.

I recommend daily entries knowing full well that only a marooned castaway with nothing else to do could be religious enough to write every day. I commend anyone who can accomplish this in real life. Your destinies probably won't be known to you any sooner because you journal daily, but the regularity is good for your mind and spirit just as regularity is healthful to many human processes.

Examine your schedule as explained earlier and formulate a plan, then stick to it, whatever you have to do. But how do you motivate yourself to be a regular journal writer?

A school principal once told me that the public schools are doing a fantastic job at teaching the social concept of positive self-esteem. So good that the same kids who had bad grades continue to have bad grades, but now they walk around saying,

"My grades are in the can, but *I'm a really great kid!*" I chuckled before we went on to discuss the source of motivation in people.

We happened to be watching his school's basketball team while having this discussion about what it takes to be motivated. The coach had obviously done an excellent job and the team played fairly and with accuracy, winning the game.

We talked about those kids in school who participate in activities like sports or yearbook. This principal motivated his students with rules to encourage discipline, saying that they had to maintain a certain high grade-point average in order to be on teams and in clubs. We could argue forever on the merits and demerits of such a system, but we all know that school and real life are set up to reward those who excel through discipline and work, but those people are always motivated to do this. The principal said his plan had "really turned around several of the kids." The ones who wanted to play basketball.

This clean-playing, high-scoring basketball team made it into the tournament season, and I again went to the game. The new opposing team had been motivated in a completely different manner. Their mantra was "win at any cost." There was blatant pushing off, foul language on the court, kicking and general chicanery that held down the principal's well-trained, disciplined team.

They lost because they were too young to maintain their composure under difficult circumstances. This they can learn. The memory of the loss will serve as a motivation down the road for each player. That night they were severely disappointed. Some will work harder and some will quit.

Where does motivation come from when you are crushed by unfairness in spite of your truthfulness, skill and discipline? It comes from the universal wellspring of hope. The hope that in some way we will each make some kind of difference in the world before we die. The hope that we will make a positive contribution to the human condition.

For this young basketball team, the motivation was winning the tournament AND maintaining a good grade-point average. Good lessons for anyone. So why do some continue after losing a game and some quit? Because of an identity crisis.

Even the principal with his well-meaning good grades requirement contributed to each player's misunderstanding of the truth about who they really are. Basketball is what they do, not the truth of *who they are.* The schools, parents, newspapers and friends see them as players in a win-lose situation instead of boys who had done their absolute best for the moment.

Too much attention is given to what someone does instead of who they are inside. Players of any age, of any game should be recognized for their gifts as people. Win or lose, a ballgame from the past cannot ever substitute for self-discipline in the present moment. The good-hearted principal wants the best for his students. Positive reinforcement of each student's individuality will hold that student upright longer than memories of the past.

The students whose grades "are in the can" instinctively know that their grades, while important, don't symbolize who they are on a deep level. They *are* great kids because they have refused to be known for their grades, and are instead recognized for the potential to make a positive impression on the world. Everywhere I've ever been, smiles go a lot further than grade transcripts.

So, how do you maintain your motivation to journal? By accepting what you accomplish each time you journal as a small step along the way to being a positive contribution to the journey of us all.

Here are some ideas for accepting what time you have to dedicate to journaling:

1. Plan your journal writing in manageable chunks. If your plan is to journal for five days of the week, try a visual game of creating a map on a large sheet of colored construction paper. Cut five symbolic pictures from magazines and paste them along a "route" stretching from one side of the paper to the other. DON'T WRITE ANY DAYS OR DATES IN! Instead, write under each picture the date on which you accomplish the journaling. For every successful day, draw a line like on a road map connecting the pictures until you reach your destination. At the conclusion of successfully completing five journal entries in one week, celebrate. You can depict the celebration in advance by cutting out more pictures from magazines that show what you have planned when you meet the goal and the deadline.

2. Arrange with a friend to call or e-mail a reminder to you to journal. Pre-arrange the days you want the contact and only do this for a couple of weeks. Include your friend in the end-of-week celebration to satisfy his/her need for encouragement!

3. What's important to you? Journal about this question many times and you will eventually see a pattern that will help answer it. The people,

principles and fundamentals that are genuinely important, that is something you hold dear and would rather see prosper than suffer, are the entities that ultimately serve as your incentives. In down times, they are your private lifelines back to up time. They keep you going. What are they? Who are they? Where are they? Why are they important to you? Identify and commit this information to your journal and refer to it when you need motivation.

WRITER WELLNESS CORNERSTONES

* Successful journaling means a consistent schedule and honest writing.

* Motivate yourself to journal on a regular basis by accepting each entry as a small step along your journey.

"My Expectations for This Journal"

The word "rule" is a descendent of the Latin word *regere* meaning "to lead straight." When my precocious five-year-old asked me why there were rules, I explained that rules were a form of protection. They keep people from hurting themselves or others. Of course, that didn't end it there. She then took the protection rule into her own impression of reality and decided that if she wasn't doing anybody any "harm" by covering her legs with diaper rash ointment like it was suntan lotion and sitting on the carpet to watch television, that should be all right. Anyone who's ever wondered why there are rules has considered breaking them.

While there are accepted laws and regulations in our society, I don't have to *like* them, but I should *appreciate* them and abide...as much as I can. But one of the first things you'll hear or read about people who are "there" (i.e., published), is that they went against some custom or rule to know their success.

And this is where I give you permission to ignore the rules as you write in your journal and allow yourself to be led by a different faith, the faith bubbling around inside of you. I despise cliché, no matter how often I use it, but the simple rule is to trust the faith within yourself for the best results when journaling.

When I look inside, I see myself in my favorite lavender printed flannel pajamas sitting in a gloriously plush reclining lounger with a peaceful glow and a grand smile on my face. Pajamas are my favorite clothing. I'm relaxing back in this comfy chair while the other me is skipping erratically around in a circle trying to get into that chair in the center of the deranged circle dance I'm performing. The peaceful, easygoing, got-it-together me is teasing the uptight, judgmental, disorganized me to let go of the rules and flop down in an easy chair and write. By the way, the more I journal, the smaller the circle becomes and the closer I get to melding my personal dichotomies. Some would say I'm dancing around my own enlightenment, but I'm sure I'm just trying to be my own best friend. Maybe that's what the whole personal journey is: Being one's own best friend or having faith that you are a good person and trusting yourself to demonstrate that in everyday life and interactions. But I digress.

The more I journal sans boundaries, the freer my creative spirit is to accept the processes and the products as necessary to the creation. I'm more able to appreciate the rules that restricted my talents and more understanding of the fact that learning the restrictions and choosing to leap over them is part of the artistic learning stages.

In the journal I actively promote a venue where I have total freedom of choice, the most fundamental of human rights, to be whatever, whoever, whenever I want. But this is just an exercise in writing. The sensation of liberation is what I carry over into creative projects from the examinations and ruminations I experience in my journal.

There are times when I write something down that I'm ashamed of. Instead of judging myself or setting a boundary that disallows the writing of such feelings and thoughts, I forge it to the page then burn it. Literally. I rip out the papers that hold the words of an ugliness I need to get over and burn them in the barbecue in the back yard. And my meanness stinks while it's burning and I sniff it in and tell myself that it's OVER. I don't have this problem as an issue in my life any longer. If it really smells, I bury the ashes far from the house, the place I love, live and laugh. It works. Try it at least once.

Above all, don't let your crazy, disorganized self set the controls of how you will journal. There are no Journal Police out to see if you are abiding by the rules of grammar, polite language, construction, etc. Recline your heart in an easy chair and let it happen on its own.

Here are some ideas for having faith in your journal writing.

1. Plan *when* you are going to journal, not *what* you are going to write. Use a variety of tools like daily affirmation books, runes or books written especially to provide you with ideas for journal entries. When responding to a question or idea, first copy the prompt word for word, using quotation marks if you like to remind yourself later that your words are a response. Read through the sentence or phrase again and again until some word or part stimulates you to think of something else. It will usually be something pertinent to your life and this will get you going. Write, write, write everything you want about the issue in your life and when you feel the pace falling off, look back quickly at the prompt and see how it ends. Try to tie the ending of your response to the conclusion of the prompt and make a decision if possible. A conclusion or final decision is not the integral part. Examining the question in writing and opening yourself to the *many* possibilities at your disposal to deal with the problem is the important part of the exercise.

2. Incarcerate the judge. It's big news when a fine, upstanding judge gets thrown into jail, but that's where all hopeless complainers belong. This is an artistic exercise meant to help you visualize your personal critic behind bars when you need him/her there. You need paper and colorful markers. Draw the cage. Envision the constraint you see yourself in but don't put your image there. Instead, spend time on the details of the confines so you have a picture to refer to until it becomes a permanent mental image you can call upon at will when you need to lock up your faultfinding, nitpicking, derogatory, pain-in-the-ass censor who keeps you from touching your true creative wealth. I had to imagine a chain link fence overgrown with bright purple flowers surrounding me before I could complete this exercise. I detailed the drawing into my journal pages more than once. It continues to represent the place I secure Mr.-That's-Not-Right when I need creative freedom. He's strong and he shakes the bars, but only I have the key, and he doesn't get out until I'm done working. I'm a humanitarian. My critic gets out occasionally on "work release."

3. These are some titles I recommend for finding good sources of journal prompts:

Blum, Ralph H. and Susan Loughan, *The Healing Runes,* St. Martin's Press, New York, 1995.

Fishel, Ruth, *Time For Joy,* Health Communications, Inc., Deerfield Beach, Florida, 1988.

Fitzgerald, Astrid, editor, *An Artist's Book of Inspiration*, Lindisfarne Press, Hudson, New York, 1996.

Gracian, Baltasar, *The Art of Worldly Wisdom,* translated by Christopher Maurer, Doubleday, New York, 1992.

Herman, Emily and Jennifer Richard Jacobson, *Stones from the Muse*, Fireside, New York, 1997.

Hughes, Elaine Farris, *Writing from the Inner Self*, HarperCollins Publishers, New York, 1991.

Lawson, David, *The Eye of Horus, An Oracle of Ancient Egypt,* St. Martin's Press, New York, 1996.

Niven, David, Ph.D., *The 100 Simple Secrets of Happy People,* HarperCollins Publishers, New York, 2000.

Reeves, Judy, *A Writer's Book of Days,* New World Library, Novato, California, 1999.

Zukav, Gary, *Thoughts From The Seat of the Soul, Meditations for Souls in Process,* Fireside, New York, 1989.

Ruiz, Don Miguel, *The Four Agreements Wisdom Book,* Amber-Allen Publishing, Inc., San Rafael, California, 1997.

Ruiz, Don Miguel, *The Four Agreements Companion Book,* Amber-Allen Publishing, Inc., San Rafael, California, 2000.

Warner, Carolyn, *Treasury of Women's Quotations,* Prentice Hall, Englewood Cliffs, New Jersey, 1992.

And don't misinterpret all of this hoopla about journaling as a replacement for your writing projects. Writing in a journal or diary is an adjunct activity to your efforts at creating stories, poems, songs, paintings, etc. Journal writing will keep the writing fires burning when you haven't got the ideas or impulses you need to work on a piece.

Journal as regularly as possible and keep the habit, even while you are working hard on a manuscript, play or whatever. Even a few minutes a day will result in the unique perspective and the driving energy you crave to keep you going on a project.

On the flip side, journal writing keeps you writing, creating, and satisfied when the projects aren't happening as fast as you'd like.

WRITER WELLNESS CORNERSTONES

* You are free to be your true self in your journal.

* You may forget the rules of grammar, polite conversation and sentence structure when you journal.

* Carry the sense of liberation over into your creative works but abide within the artistic confines of your art.

How Will Journal Writing Help?

When I was ten years old, my best friend stayed overnight at my house and saw my diary. She picked it up and read it, then told everyone at school what I said about my family, boys I thought were cute and other details that, at the time, were very personal. I was devastated. Today I wouldn't want anything like that to happen again, but I never record my thoughts, plans, dreams, wishes and complaints without an overriding understanding that the entries will most likely be read by others *someday*. My daughters will probably be the most interested because they are the most curious. I take precautions to protect my journals to prolong the inevitable. Someone else IS going to read my personal writings someday. I aim to control what day that happens.

The protection of the actual journals has to do with where I keep them and how secure the location. It involves a lock and key that absolutely no one, except me, has access to. They can't get at my diaries without a hacksaw or a locksmith's help. This way I have no restrictions whatsoever on what I write in the journals, and that's the way it has to be to assure the best results. There can be no boundaries on what I write in order to get the most thorough internal cleansing.

It's the mental and emotional housecleaning that I recommend journal writing for, especially if you need clarity when you create. And every artist *needs* clarity when they invent, but not every artist incorporates internal cleansing into the artistic process.

For example, after many, many years of recording my life's events and dreams, I am writing this section without having first completed my morning ritual of journal writing. It's an experiment that is yielding exactly the results I expected. That is: lack of flow, difficulty choosing the right words, misspellings, trouble with continuity and an inability to make decisions about the simplest of grammatical questions. Why do I think the same is happening to you when you attempt creativity before or completely without the disinfecting process of journal writing? The simple answer is experience, both personal and those of writing students who have tried this for themselves.

But will it work for you? The written word is a potent tool. It contributes to change and to education in ways the spoken word can only wish for.

Writing in your journal will have a definite impact on your life. Kathleen Adams, founder of The Center for Journal Therapy says, "The power of writing is accessible to anyone who desires self-directed change. It requires no special talent, skills or experience—only a willingness to explore moments of ecstasy and moments of despair, critical illness and crucial life choice, psychological healing and spiritual discovery."

On the front of a popular publication devoted to the art and science of keeping a diary these words perpetually appear: improve, memoir, breakthrough, goals, and connecting. Why are these concepts important to journal writing and creativity? Because they are signs of flow, of "being in the groove," of achieving the "zone," of meeting oneself on the path where you are inventing yourself everyday. This spot is much easier to dance in if there is no clutter from your life to step around while you move to the music that only you can hear.

WRITER WELLNESS CORNERSTONES

* Great effort should be put into keeping your journals safe from unwanted readers.

* Journal writing is specifically aimed at mental and emotional housecleaning which clears the way for you to think about creative projects.

* To be void of mental and emotional traumas is the best way to connect faster and cleaner with your creative flow.

How Will Journal Writing Help?
Exercises
(* set a timer)

JOURNAL

Safety. There are no Journal Police. Therefore, there is no one to protect your journals or to critique what you write in them either. But your paranoia still exists. And fear is the source. Fear of what? That's what you must journal about now. One or all one thousand fears. Write about what you fear and try to find a reason. Honesty counts. But only you will know. (* 15 minutes)

EXERCISE

Almost everyone is uncomfortable going backwards. Backing up the car, walking backwards, and goddess forbid, turning upside down while going backwards. In every case, it's fear of the unknown. (* 5 minutes)

Work with your backward phobias in these "daring" ways.

1. Walk backwards 20 steps.
2. Hang upside down and backwards off the side of your bed for up to one minute.
3. Prow of the Ship. Put both hands behind you and grasp a counter or doorknob of a closed door. Without letting go, walk away a few step and place put your feet side by side. Arch your back gently by pushing both hips forward and slightly lifting your chin. The entire front of your body should make an easy curve from head to ankles. Breathe! Come out slowly after four or five breaths.

RELAX

Aromatherapy studies have proven the relaxing, soothing qualities of lavender essential oil. Take a warm bath laden with 12-20 drops of lavender oil. Light a lavender scented candle if you want and turn the lights low. Sprinkle a few drops of lavender oil onto your bath towel and pop it into the dryer before your bath for an added sensation when you dry off.

NUTRITION

Look through at least three cookbooks borrowed from the library or a friend. Don't use your own. Choose, prepare and eat three dishes you've never tried before. Keep one for your new life menu.

CREATE

This is a weekend project or can be worked on a little each day for a week. It's best to focus on the process for whatever time it takes. You can sit in front of the television while you choose and cut out pictures or keep several magazines in the car. While you are waiting for someone to get out of school, work, or piano lessons, rip pages out that have pictures you want to include on your collage.

Spend about two hours going through magazines and cutting out images about fear and safety issues that matter to you. Make a collage with these pictures and let it sit for a day or two.

Return to the collage with your journal, ample time, and pen in hand. As you review the images, make a word list of everything you see and feel. Depending on the pictures you've chosen, your list could include words like heights, dark, loneliness, afraid, lost or sick. Continue this list until nothing more pops into your head.

This procedure also works to jumpstart writing projects.

I had a magazine article due and was having trouble finding the lead I wanted. Several days of writing lead paragraphs didn't lend the right one. The deadline loomed. It was my first time writing for the publication and I didn't want a bad start by missing the deadline.

I decided to set aside the article and use work time to create a large collage with every magazine picture I could find in two hours that had even the slightest association with my article topic. It worked.

The next day, all my stumbling gave way to flowing ideas that the editor glowed about in a later e-mail, and almost nothing was changed about my original copy. The best comments were about clean copy, well-written, arriving AHEAD OF DEADLINE!

CREATIVE-WHILE-YOU-WORK IDEAS

I know cotton and linen handkerchiefs are difficult to find these days, but they are still out there. I have regularly found them in dollar stores, the men's area of department stores, antique stores, specialty gift shops and catalogs.

Buy a handkerchief and drop three to six drops of lavender oil on it, then put it into your purse. Or take the bottle of oil to work. When you need a clear head for a meeting or project, take out the hanky or bottle and hold either about six inches from your nose. Take three long breaths, inhaling the soothing aroma. Tip: Keep the hanky in a zippered storage bag to maintain and lengthen the scent.

EXERCISE

Fitness for Writers and Other Creative Sorts

Like most writers, I love words and when I see the word "exercise" I think of looking up the word's spelling in the dictionary. You know the ultimate question here. How can I look up the word if I don't how to spell it? And how can people exercise correctly if they don't know how to do it? I'm sure this inadequacy is why most people don't exercise regularly, and what prompted the invention of the spell check in word processing programs. Some techno geek was fed up with his father saying, "Look it up in the dictionary," and not knowing where to start.

Fitness is a mega-business in this country, but so far the marketing has only been truly successful at alerting people to the existence of fitness equipment, videotapes, classes, and books. We still have a frightening obesity rate, and the disease diabetes, most often found in overweight individuals, is the fastest growing malady of our times.

I've been part of the fitness movement for my entire life. My mother was one of the very first women certified to teach aerobic dancing in this country in the late seventies. She came back from her training clinic saying, "Nobody *wants* to work that hard. I'll never get anybody in these classes."

As usual, she was ahead of the pack. West Virginians didn't know aerobic dancing was anything different from square dancing, and they were already busy two nights a week with that. True, many square dancers break a decent sweat, but somehow it's not the same.

Mom kept those fitness classes on the schedule beside tap, ballet and acrobatics, and the students finally arrived, until the class we had to rent a basketball court to teach all 200 of the ladies who enrolled! My sister had taken over the reins of that particular department by then and the program continued to be a strong moneymaker for us both until disco. But I digress.

The point to take here is that fads come and go, but body fat is really difficult to get to go unless you have a good program and the discipline to follow it. For most people that means simplicity and support, the two main elements contained in the ideas for keeping creative people like writers, artists, painters, graphic designers, singers, actors, sculptors, jewelry makers—well, you get the picture, physically fit.

Why do most people want to be physically fit or at least physically active in a productive way? To feel better. What's wrong with how you feel? "I don't feel balanced. I don't feel good. I have no energy. But I don't know what to do, and I probably can't afford the equipment or the classes."

And there are those who don't believe that their health contributes to their quality of life or their level of creativity. In 1996 the Surgeon General released the first ever report on physical activity and health. The conclusions should lead you to understand that physical activity is literally a matter of life or the death of life.

* Low levels of activity, resulting in fewer calories used than consumed, contribute to the high prevalence of obesity in the United States.

* Physical activity may favorably affect body fat distribution.

* People of all ages, both male and female, benefit from regular physical activity.

* More than 60 percent of American adults are not regularly physically active. In fact, 25 percent of all adults are not active at all.

* Significant health benefits can be obtained by including a moderate amount of physical activity on most, if not all, days of the week.

* Additional health benefits can be gained through greater amounts of physical activity.

* Physical activity reduces the risk of premature mortality in general, and of coronary heart disease, hypertension, colon cancer, and diabetes mellitus in particular.

* Physical activity also improves mental health and is important for muscles, bones, and joints.

(The Surgeon General's "Report on Physical Activity and Health," 1996. is available for $22 from the Superintendent of Documents, P.O. Box 371954, Pittsburgh, PA 15250-7954, (202) 512-1800, 7:30 a.m.-4:30 p.m. ET.)

You first have to decide that you *want* to be in better shape. Is being physically fit important to you? Look around and simply decide if you want to stay alive a good while longer enjoying the friends, family and fabric of life you're living, or do you want to enjoy those perks for less time? People who keep their bodies in good condition live longer and enjoy a better life. It's quality of life that provides the playground for your creativity.

Sure, you could go on being sickly and keep writing something that might sell someday, but this is where you give this book to your niece for a graduation present. "She has time to do this," you think. "I can't do this." It's probably more like you don't *want* to expend the energy getting into better physical and mental shape because you're not convinced that it makes any difference to your creative work. Let's look at a test case.

Shelia T. (not her real name) wrote a big book, a contemporary novel that took me and two others a chunk of time to critique for her. While it was a good story, it was just too incredibly long to be enjoyable. We discussed cutting this part and that, but she couldn't see her way clear to prune the branches we felt made the story too bulky. We loved the characters, the drama, the conflicts, the mysteries, and Shelia's writing, but the length turned us off as readers.

Shelia enrolled in Writer Wellness Workshop for six weeks and set her novel aside while we wrote in journals, played creativity games, exercised, and read titles by inspirational author SARK. Shelia was hesitant about the workshop because of a two-year-old knee injury. Depression about her lack of mobility and constant pain kept her from seeing things clearly in many areas of her life.

But Shelia was disciplined about responding in her journal to the prompts I provided, and she learned to adapt the yoga exercises taught in class to accommodate her disability. Every week she would bring in her journal entries and creativity project assignments and participate in the yoga and deep relaxation exercises.

Each workshop student completes a lengthy questionnaire at the first class. They must write everything that comes to mind in response to the questions. The pages cover the student's current lifestyle, desires, and goals for the future. The answers tell me what a student really does with her life and what she really wants out of life.

Shelia responded to "What do YOU want?" like this:

"I want to be healthy and to hike in the woods. (The last physical therapist I had laughed when I stated that as my goal. That is why she will be the last PT I have. It may take time, but I am stubborn and patient.)"

"I want to be a novelist. I want to make my living writing. I want to have all the time I want to write. I want to be home when my children get out of school and go to all their special occasions. I do not need to be rich. Just make enough to pay the bills."

Shelia participated in workshop with awareness and dedication, and eventually realized several of her wants from the above list. A cherished family member died during Shelia's time in workshop, but she journaled about the funeral and her family and she never missed a class.

Shelia journals regularly now because of the workshop. She received a rational diagnosis about her knee and exercises in a warm therapeutic swimming pool on a weekly basis. Now she can stand up long enough to help prepare dinner for her family. She looked at her novel from a somewhat healthier perspective and turned it into a three-book family saga of reasonable proportion that is circulating among agents and publishers.

Lastly, Shelia quit her computer programming job which irritated her body and her mind, and now operates a successful manuscript critique business from her home where ninety percent of her clients come in through her self-designed Web site on the Internet. She is paying all of her bills as she works within her dream. We still work together, and while she still has a way to go to improve her health, Shelia's life is answering her desires because she committed herself and her family to the same wish in writing and with action.

Physical exercise was Shelia's greatest challenge because of her knee injury, but she allowed the disability of one part of her body to control the rest of her life until she took the time to examine her true desires through journal work.

The simple act of commending the words to paper inspires the universe to cooperate with our minds and hearts to allow our dreams to find us. In the dream-granting department, the universe has one rule: You cannot tell the universe exactly *how* to grant your wish, only exactly what it is you wish for. Too many restrictions on a dream mean that you don't really want it to happen because conditions have nothing to do with true love. And the universe truly loves you. It just needs unbridled liberties in order to serve your desires.

So how does exercise factor into realizing your heart's desires? Your body is your vehicle. It's your only way of being a part of your dream when the universe gets the pieces all in a row for you. If you don't have the physical form in good condition, you can't participate fully in your dreams. And when your body is conditioned, it responds better to everything, and it is especially supportive of your emotional state of mind. When you *feel* better physically, you *feel* better emotionally and you are better suited to realizing the full potential of your dreams.

I promote walking and yoga. There is something for everyone within those two types of exercise if they make the effort. No exercise will *do* anything for you. You are responsible for employing the effort and finding the unique place where you can prosper and fulfill your body's needs. I'm well aware of everything else available in the fitness world. More power to you if you choose and can see overall benefits from anything else. The goal is to keep your body moving. Don't rule out walking and yoga as complimentary programs. They are adaptable, inexpensive and worthwhile.

Also important to your wellness makeover is the concept of stress reduction. A certain amount of stress is acceptable, but many of us go way over the load limit when it comes to daily life stresses through no fault of our own. Most of the time, you can journal and talk with your spouse and family about helping reduce the amount of stress in your life. Delegating simple chores to others can greatly reduce the responsibility burdens that interfere with your creative flow. However, it's just as important to learn to deal with stress on terms that allow you to control it. Yes, you can, over time, teach yourself a completely different set of physical and mental responses to stress. It won't happen overnight, but it is very possible. And easy. You have all the tools built in, and the choice is completely yours.

WRITER WELLNESS CORNERSTONES

* An exercise program requires your dedication and discipline to follow it.

* A good fitness program is simple to maintain and supportive of your health goals.

* Quality of life provides the playground for your creativity.

* Commit your fitness dreams to paper and they will be easier to realize.

* Your body is your vehicle. It helps you be an active part of your creative dreams.

* The fundamentals of fitness are regular moderate exercise and applied stress reduction practices.

Fitness For Writers And Other Creative Sorts
Exercises
(* set a timer)

JOURNAL

Journal honestly about your physical health. Spend whatever words necessary complaining and complimenting your fitness level. Have you ever felt good physically? When? Why or why not? Explore the issue of exercise with integrity and you'll eventually find a true feeling through the writing. Write in response to what you hear in your head, and a kernel of useful information will make itself known to you. You'll have something tangible to work with while recharging your life with exercise. (* 30 minutes)

EXERCISE

Take a twenty-minute walk EVERY DAY for a week at approximately the same time each day. Journal about how you feel before and after each walk, and before and after the week. A single sentence is enough. Make a pact with yourself to incorporate walking into your fitness plan. (* 20 minutes)

RELAX

Peace in. Stress out. Lie on your back in a comfortable, supported position. Close your eyes. Take three deep, slow breaths. Now breathe normally through your nostrils.

With every inhale, repeat to yourself, "Peace in." With every exhale, repeat to yourself, "Stress out." (* 10 minutes)

NUTRITION

Many people avoid exercise because of the fear that exercise will increase their appetites (which it will, but it also increases your healthy metabolism rate), and that if they want to lose weight they'll have to deny themselves the pleasures of food. Or more correctly, the flavors they associate with eating: fat, salt, and sugar.

Fat, salt, and sugar are added to "convenience" foods that are quick to prepare and eat. Shop differently. Not just at the grocery store, but in restaurants.

AVOID: partially hydrogenated vegetable oil and high fructose corn syrup.

DON'T ADD: salt

SUBSTITUTE: honey, lemon juice, low-salt soy sauce, garlic powder, onion flakes, oil and vinegar.

CREATE

My Shape Book. Children in schools are encouraged to write in a number of fun, interesting ways. One is called creating shape books where the shape of the book cover, inside paper and theme of the story are all related. For example: A story about a cat is written on paper cut into the shape of a cat with the front and back covers also in the shape of a cat. This is decorated to look like a cat.

Devoting yourself to a new fitness plan will ultimately gift you with a new body shape and a new perspective. The point of making shape books with kids is to keep them focused on a single theme in their writing. It also bolsters creativity and satisfaction to produce a fully realized project. Your "shape" book about fitness can do the same thing for you: Focus, creativity and satisfaction will support you every exercise step of the way.

Design and create a shape book about your fitness goals, plans and results. Have fun and be imaginative but produce a functional booklet that contributes seriously to your process.

Some shape ideas: barbells, sneakers, bicycle, or a person shape. Cut out the front and back covers from construction paper or card stock. Decorate and title.

Use the cover to trace around and cut out paper for the inside.

Bind with a paper rad (those metal things you poke through paper and spread the two prongs apart, a.k.a. metal fasteners), or punch holes and string yarn or ribbon through, or just staple it.

You have a shape book about your shape dreams!

(Tip: Ready-made shape book patterns are available from school supply stores and catalogs, craft and scrap booking shops.)

CREATIVE-WHILE-YOU-WORK IDEAS

Workdays are hectic. Somewhere there has to be a moment just for you. In all probability, your employer *wants* you to be healthy and satisfied because you will be a more productive employee who misses less work due to illness, fatigue or injury. The statistics on this back me up.

The law supports the issue of reasonable breaks and meal times. Do an Internet search on the labor laws for your state and you will find, as I did, that an employer must grant up to a twenty-minute break for every four to six hours that you work. Lunch periods must be at least thirty minutes in most states. There are not federal laws regulating this, but there are U.S.

Department of Labor guidelines that states are supposed to adhere to with their labor laws.

You are justly entitled to some private, uninterrupted time while at work, and you can use the time for restoration and food. This includes exercise.

It's you who must make the decision and the choice to find ways to gain health and satisfaction while you're at work. The law allows for the time. You must use it wisely.

Write up an exercise schedule complete with times, exercises and locations. Schedule yourself to exercise briefly at work for a month. Give yourself a gold star for every day you meet your mini exercise goal. See if you don't feel better in a month. Several other employees might follow your model as well.

Here are some Web addresses to get you started:

www.gottrouble.com/legal

www.freeadvice.com

www.chicagolegalnet.com

www.dol.gov/elaws/brouse.asp (U.S. Department of Labor)

www.state.wv.us/labor/

An Exercise Schedule

A proper, long term and moderate exercise program is the foundation of a wellness way of life. You find a program through research and trying it out. Fifty percent of adults who fail in maintaining their desired weight do so because they don't exercise enough. (Source: The Calorie Control Council National Consumer Survey, 2000)

Long term and moderate are the operative words. Sure, we know lots of people who have been distance running, aerobic dancing or pole-vaulting for years, but their days of intense pavement smacking are numbered.

My experience is from the dance studio. Football players take it easy on an injury. Dancers wrap it and go back to class until it doesn't work any longer. Thankfully, my mother and ballet teacher knew a different route. We've directed a studio for over fifty years and haven't had any more than tendonitis and some blisters on students or ourselves. The key is proper stretching (like hatha yoga) and diet.

Physical exercise is typically a cleansing process the body appreciates and needs. It also burns calories, increases your metabolic rate, decreases the appetite in some individuals, produces positive psychological benefits, decreases stress and increases a person's overall well being. (Calorie Control Council)

It's best to exercise while the sun is in the sky, but if your schedule doesn't permit this, choose the time before eating dinner on weeknights and slightly earlier in the day on the weekends when your time should be more flexible. Caution: Your body loves consistency in exercise and diet. It will quickly adapt to your regular routine and show long-term benefits if you keep your schedule on track. Exercise as close to the same time each day as possible.

WRITER WELLNESS CORNERSTONES

* Exercise is more productive over the long term if it is moderate and suited to your current fitness level.

* The body appreciates the cleansing process associated with exercise.

* Exercise as close to the same time each day as possible.

An Exercise Schedule
Exercises

JOURNAL

Write a letter to yourself promising to stick to your exercise schedule. Put it in an envelope, address it to yourself, stamp it and take it to a post office after 5:00 p.m. Since mail taken to the post office this late doesn't go out until the next day, it will give you an extra day for the letter to return and time to complete the exercise program.

While the letter is boomeranging back to you, exercise. When it returns, paste the letter and envelope into your journal and write about how you stayed on the exercise schedule (or not).

EXERCISE

Slow and steady. A lifetime exercise regimen is about long-term, consistent results. Commit yourself to a month of daily walking for fifteen minutes a day, six days a week. I know a month seems like an eternity, but it's a manageable amount of time to evaluate at the end.

Write about how you felt before and after the walk. That's all. Three sentences every day.

"Head cluttered and thoughts muddled."

"Walked ten blocks in fifteen minutes."

"Able to think clearly, more relaxed, smiling!"

RELAX

Use your daily relaxation practice to release stress over a specific situation. Perhaps a personality, unresolved argument or irritating responsibility is causing you to react negatively. Apply relaxation practice to help you overcome the stress associated with the problem.

Begin the session with three deep, slow breaths, then bring the offense to mind. Immediately start a mental mantra repeating the same phrase for every breath over and over in your mind. Doing this for five minutes while you allow the problem to waiver through your consciousness guarantees you a softening about the issue, and most importantly, you are able to achieve a symbolic detachment from the issue. This allows you to choose to respond peacefully to the stresses of real life.

It doesn't answer or end the problem; it provides another choice, one of compassion for yourself and the dilemma. Less stress allows you to be open to alternative solutions. With more solutions, you have less stress.

Choose one mantra per problem:

"Peace in. Harmony out."
"Peace in. Tranquility out."
"Peace in. Serenity out."
"Love in. Love out."
"Let go. Move on."
"Positive in. Negative out."
"Bliss in. Energy out."

NUTRITION

Brain dinner. Your brain relies on the full range of B vitamins for energy, productivity and tissue production. Try this simple brain dinner high in B vitamins, then include these items in your normal food consumption.

Spinach salad with one boiled egg and vinaigrette dressing.

Turkey, 4-6 ounces of boneless breast or lean ground turkey breast broiled or pan-fried in 2 tablespoons of olive oil.

Brown rice, steamed or boiled, hearty helping.

Bread spread with peanut butter or almond butter.

Dried fruit without sulfites.

CREATE

Support your mind's spatial awareness. Find, borrow or buy a set of children's building blocks. Stack, sort, arrange and build with them until a structure "happens."

Now take pencil and drawing paper and sketch your building as three dimensionally as you can. Color with pencils or markers.

CREATIVE-WHILE-YOU-WORK IDEAS

I live in a downtown neighborhood surrounded with businesses ranging from a balloon shop to the federal government. Employees walk by my house in a perpetual stream at virtually the same time every workday of the week.

I see nurses in scrubs swinging small hand weights, gentlemen in suits whose ties flap from the pace, and even a chiropractor who closes his office for a daily two hour lunch to run three miles faster than I can type.

Many faces have become familiar to me over the years as these steady fellows cruise by my house in their work clothes and tennis shoes. We wave to each other. Very few ever stop and chat. They are on a mission and a deadline. They have to get their exercise in for the day and back to the office on time.

The city government offices, hospital employees and federal workers have printed and distributed maps explaining routes, distances and time required for midday walk breaks. It's really caught on until the sedate inner city housing sidewalks are literally teaming with enthusiastic walkers and runners. This is possible anywhere.

There are several places you can inquire to see if a plan exists or how to get one started in your work district.

Contact hospitals, the YMCA, and the YWCA first. Their mission statements usually call for community exercise awareness, and if they don't have something in place, a program director probably has the details to help get one started.

Malls are the next place to contact. Many malls and hospitals have indoor walking clubs. They can tell you who put it together for them.

Perhaps there's an exercise establishment in your workplace neighborhood who would be interested in helping organize and promote a daily exercise program for local employees.

Or chart out several paths yourself, draw up maps and distribute them at work. Include a sign-up sheet for those who want to walk as clans.

Hatha Yoga for Writers

The most portable, accessible, inexpensive and long-term exercise in the world is hatha yoga. The phrase "hatha yoga" is from the ancient Sanskrit language. Hatha means "sun and moon." Yoga means "union." Hatha yoga is the joining of opposites. Yes, there is stretching (never bouncing!), but hatha yoga includes structured breathing, calm mental focus, working within the physical range of motion of the student and relaxation. It fits anybody wherever they may be physically and mentally.

Videos and books on yoga, while easily available, can't help you with the details specific to your individual challenges like a good teacher. I recommend one in the beginning for everyone, but no teacher, regardless of how encouraging, can replace your own desire to be fit and healthy. The "deep want" has to come from inside you. If you have that, the patience and dedication will be there for a competent instructor to guide.

STANDING MOUNTAIN POSE

Fig. 1

With your mind's eye, mentally observe a strong, quiet mountain reaching upward through the clouds. Stand on a level surface with both feet parallel and hip width apart. Roll your shoulders slightly up, back and down to open your chest. Gently tuck your tailbone under and check your body for postural alignment.

Are you standing erect but relaxed with every body part, including your head, in a comfortable line? If so, inhale as you raise both arms overhead and reach through your fingertips. Exhale slowly and easily, and hold the arms above for four to five slow, easy breaths. (Fig. 1)

To finish, inhale and lift the arms higher above your head and allow them to float down easily as you exhale. If you have too much tension in your neck, keep your arms lowered to your sides until you are stronger. Increase your practice until you can hold this posture for one minute.

ASSISTED STANDING FORWARD BEND

Create a mental picture of a strong, wooden table with a clean, flat surface.

Fig. 2

Standing behind a chair, position feet parallel and hip width apart. Rest both hands on the back of the chair. Keeping feet parallel, slowly walk backwards from the chair until your upper body is in line with the floor (horizontal). Look at the floor and allow your head to float between your arms. Your ears are lined up with your upper arms. Breathe normally and consciously lengthen your spine from head to tailbone by exhaling and flattening your back at the same time. Do not allow your belly to droop toward the ground and sway your backbone. Keep "growing" your spine from the hips through the top of your head for four to five breaths. (Fig. 2)

Allow an inhale to walk you forward to the chair and return to standing. Notice the new "spaces" along your spine. That slight tingle is oxygen!

SUPPORTED TREE POSE

This is a balancing posture. Balance improves many physical situations such as muscle tone and circulation, but it primarily develops confidence. While balancing is a physical challenge, the mental focus necessary is also a test of your determination. You simply cannot achieve this pose without complete mental dedication to it. Accomplishing the many levels of this posture will increase your belief in yourself in a subtle, charming way, and supply a ready source of self-assurance to apply to other areas in your life.

Start by mentally imagining yourself as a tree growing two directions simultaneously. Clear your mind of distractions with a cleansing breath. Begin Supported Tree Pose by standing beside the back of a sturdy chair. Position both feet so that toes are pointing straight ahead and heels are parallel and directly beneath your hips. Place one hand on the back of the chair, the other hand on your waist.

Fig. 3

Inhale and raise the outside leg (the one farthest from the chair back) by sliding the inside of your foot up the inside of the supporting leg. Stop raising your knee anywhere between the ankle and knee of your supporting leg. Exhale and rotate in the outside hip and turn the raised knee out, allowing the sole of your foot to rest on the inside of your supporting leg. (Fig. 3)

Take time here to focus your eyes on a fixed point in front of you and don't let them move as you hold the balance. Adjust your alignment from head to toe and raise your hand off the back of the chair. Keep breathing through your nostrils and hold your eyes perfectly still. If you can't hold yourself steady, do the exercise with one hand on the back of the chair until you grow the stamina to balance without the aid of the chair.

If you don't need the chair, place both hands on your hips and hold Tree Pose for 20 seconds. Slowly inhale and lower your leg. Practice on the other side. Increase your balance time with practice, gradually working your way up to a one-minute balance per side.

STANDING SOLAR BREATH

Just like the plants in your garden, you need sunlight and fresh air to thrive. Standing Solar Breath is great for increasing circulation, oxygen flow, flexibility and coordination of movement with breath.

Visualize a small bright white light in the center of your torso. Envision heat with this light.

Fig. 4

Stand with feet parallel, heels directly beneath the width of your hips, arms hanging at your sides. As you inhale, raise both arms straight through your sides to touch fingertips overhead. Attempt to synchronize your body movements with your breath. (Fig. 4)

Exhale while lowering arms through the sides and bending forward from the hip joints until you are folded forward as far as possible. Touch your palms together in front of your knees or shins and point the crown of your head to the floor. (Fig. 5) Synchronize your movements to last as long as your exhale. Imagine the circle of white light in your torso growing larger and hotter.

Fig. 5

Repeat the inhale, stretching upward, and exhale, folding forward six to ten times in all, each breath increasing the white heat in your body until you are completely engulfed by the warm circle of light. Dedicate this image to memory to use in situations where you feel cold or without center. With practice, a strong mental picture of the circle growing larger and hotter with each breath will be available even at times when you cannot perform the movements.

EASY SPINAL TWIST

Recall from memory what it looks like when your hands wring out a wet cloth. Notice the equal strength of both hands on either end of the cloth as well as how the wrists turn in opposite directions to accomplish the spiral of the cloth. Take a deep cleansing breath.

Sit upright in a sturdy chair without wheels on the legs. Adjust your position until your spine is totally erect, but supported by the chair, and both feet are flat on the floor. Toes are pointing straight ahead with about six inches between your feet.

Inhale, lengthening the spine upward from the tailbone while reaching both hands to the right to clasp the chair arm and/or back. Keeping the length in your spine, exhale and slowly twist your upper body to look back at the corner to your right. Lower your eyes slightly and breathe fully through the abdomen. Keep your chin level, not tilting up or down. Check that your shoulders are down away from your ears. Continue breathing. (Fig. 6)

Fig. 6

Notice any areas of tightness and use slow breathing to relax that area by consciously letting go of the muscles there. For instance, your hips, shoulders and thighs could all be tensing, but you must let them go and hold the pose. Double check that both hips are level against the chair seat and that they are pointing forward. To finish, let the breath of an inhale float your torso back to the front.

Spread your knees wide apart and slowly exhale as you roll down to hang forward between your knees. Breathe deeply four to five breaths, then float back up on an inhale to sit tall. Repeat to the left side. (Fig. 7)

Fig. 7

GENTLE STANDING SIDE STRETCH

Fig. 8

Form a mental picture of a blade of grass bending slightly in a soft breeze. This is not a deep bend or dip to the side, but an easy arching of the hip, intercostals, ribs and arm that lengthens the whole area.

Stand with feet parallel about hip distance apart. You can also do this sitting in a chair. Inhale and float both arms up through the sides to reach overhead. Exhale and clasp one wrist with the other hand and bend slightly from the waist. Use your hand to gently pull on the wrist, gradually opening the spaces between your ribs. Hold this pose, continuing to breathe four to five breaths. (Fig. 8)

Correct your alignment in this way: Keep the backs of your legs rotating out and around your leg bones, point both hips to the front and keep your outside hip from protruding to the side, don't allow any "corkscrewing" to happen in your waist or shoulder blades, attempt to open the armpit of the upper arm to increase your overhead stretch, and try to eventually align your upper arms with your ears.

To end, allow the breath of an inhale to lift your torso and arms back up to standing, then exhale as you lower both arms. Repeat on the other side, gradually working up to twenty seconds on both sides.

SEATED SPINAL LIFT

Sit on the floor with your legs stretched in front of you. Bring to mind the picture of a brightly colored hot air balloon slowly lifting from the earth into the sky. Imagine your spine gently stretching upwards.

Fig. 9

You can sit on the edge of a folded blanket if you need the support. Energize both legs by pulling the kneecaps up toward your thighs and flexing your feet (point the toes straight up). Place your palms on the floor on either side of your hips.

Inhale and press slightly with your hands into the floor while lifting your head and lengthening the full spine. Keep your elbows and knees straight while breathing four to five times. Exhale and relax. (Fig. 9)

BENT KNEE FORWARD STRETCH

Seated on the floor, bend one knee to the side, resting the sole of your foot on the inside of the other leg. Conjure up the mental picture of how a door hinge folds and opens on its stable axis. Your axis is your hip joint. Attempt to keep your spine long as you fold forward from your hip. (Fig. 10)

Fig. 10

Fig. 11

Inhale and lengthen your spine upwards through your neck. Exhale and slowly lift from your hip joints as you fold forward out over the stretched leg. Your back and hamstrings will let you know when it's time to stop folding. Hold here and breathe deeply with the abdominal muscles four to five times. (Fig. 11) End by inhaling as you sit back up. Repeat on the other leg.

There are several props to help you work your way through this posture over time. The back or "shadow" side of the body is the most resistant to change as we age. Stretching this area takes dedication and time.

Take a soft belt or strong scarf and wind your hands around the ends, then slip it under the ball of your flexed foot. Use the scarf to help "pull" you forward into the fold and to keep you at the level you desire. It's important to stretch to one point and stay there without gradually creeping back up as you hold. You can also place a blanket under the knee of the stretched leg bending it closer to you. Or a folded blanket can be placed on top of your leg to rest your forehead against.

FRESH AIR FOR YOUR LEGS

Lie on the floor on your back. Imagine the workings of a pump and how it remains connected at a central point while pumping up and down, over and over. Inhale and raise the right arm overhead and slide the left foot up until the left knee is bent for support. (Fig. 12)

Inhale and lift your right arm and leg off the floor and try to let

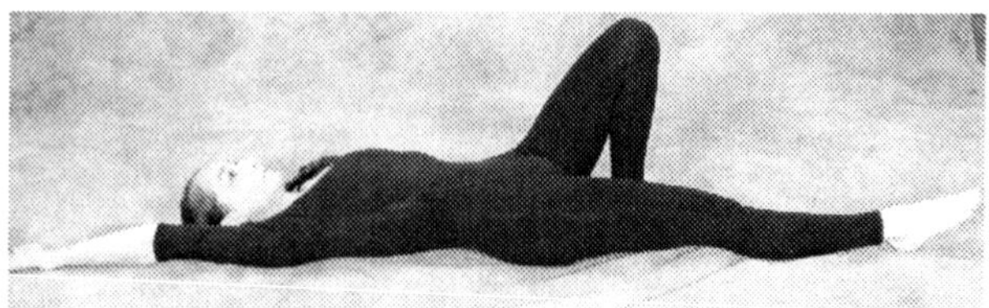
Fig. 12

them meet each other over your hip. Can you touch your leg with your fingertips? (Fig. 13) Exhale and lower your limbs. Repeat five more times on this side before changing legs. Rest after this set.

Fig. 13

Fig. 14

The next set is done with a small variation. Breathing is the same, but you lift the opposite arm and leg toward each other. (Fig. 14) Rest on your back, holding both knees into the chest after finishing this set.

LEGS UP THE WALL

This is restful pose. Find wall space where you won't knock down pictures or furniture. Think about the center of a water fountain. Note in your mind how the central column of water is fluid yet strong while it is also easy to pass your hand through. Duplicate the image of a central liquid strength in your legs as you experience this pose.

Fig. 15

Place a folded blanket on the floor right up against the wall. Sit sideways on the blanket. Keeping your hands on the floor for balance, carefully swing both legs up onto the wall as you lie down on the floor. Rest your arms, palms up, out to the sides. Move your buttocks as close to the wall as possible. Remain in this position breathing normally for up to five minutes. (Fig. 15) Close by folding your knees into your chest and holding for a few seconds before rolling over to one side and sitting up. Stay here briefly before standing up.

SPINE ROLLER

Fig. 16

Sit in your chair, feet parallel and flat on the floor. Rest your hands on your thighs. Use your mind's eye to see a cat arching its back. Keep this in mind as you roll and arch your spine.

Spine Roller increases awareness in the spine and encourages proper breath control. Inhale and raise your chin as far as you can while you push your stomach forward, making a deep curve in your back. (Fig. 16) Exhale and round over, dropping your chin forward and arching your spine. (Fig. 17)

Coordinate each undulation of the spine with the breath. Repeat six times slowly, relax.

For variation, try this movement while on all fours like a cat. It can also be done sitting on the floor in a cross-legged position.

Fig. 17

SUPPORTED TRIANGLE

This posture develops strength in the legs and increases hip flexibility. Create a scene in your mind of the great pyramids of Egypt rising solidly into the heavens, each triangular side lending stability to the other.

Fig. 18

Stand behind a chair, both hands resting on the back. Separate your feet as far as you can without slipping. Turn the toes of your right foot out to the right and turn your left foot in to the right, although not as far. Exhale and shift your left hip to the left and bend at the waist to the right. You can keep both hands on the back of the chair or inhale and raise the left hand toward the ceiling. (Fig. 18)

The stronger your legs and back become with practice, the farther you can bend to the side. Breathe fully and hold this position on each side for twenty seconds, gradually building up to one minute per side.

DEEP SLEEP ("CORPSE")

Choose a symbol that creates a restful state of mind for you. What is your dream relaxation location or image or idea? Perhaps you only need a certain color to trigger your relaxation impulse.

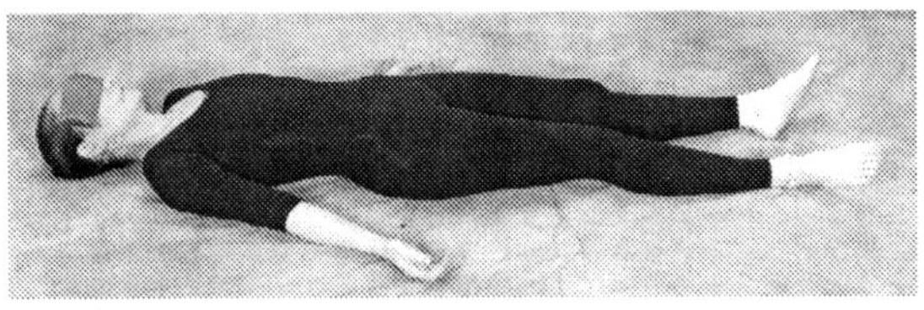

Fig. 19

This posture, also known as "corpse," is most often done lying down flat on your back on a firm surface, usually the floor, with a small blanket folded under your head. If this is absolutely impossible for you, utilize whatever props, pillows and blankets you need to lie back as far as possible and have absolutely no stress on any part of your body. (Fig. 19)

Close your eyes, take a long, deep breath in and let it out as slowly as you can. Repeat. Perform a body scan on yourself by visualizing or just thinking about different body parts and relaxing them. The simplest procedure is to begin with one foot and work your way up to your face and head. When the whole body has been relaxed, rest quietly and breathe normally for up to 10 minutes.

You can easily relax your body by thinking of a part, inhale and clench or tighten that part, then exhale and let the muscles relax. Do this for every section you can, beginning at your feet. the Deep Sleep is a traditional and functional way to end all of your yoga practices.

WRITER WELLNESS CORNERSTONES

* Hatha yoga is a Sanskrit term meaning "union of the sun and the moon," or the joining of opposites. It is a physical practice involving breathing, postures, calm mental focus and relaxation.

A Typical Yoga Workout

Fig. 20

Focus and Relax: Sit comfortably or lie down on the floor. Bring your awareness to your breath. Practice abdominal breath for five minutes. (Fig. 20)

Cat Stretch: On your hands and knees on the floor, inhale and lift your chin as you drop your stomach toward the floor. Your back should sway deeply. For added stretch, fold your toes into the floor. (Fig. 21)

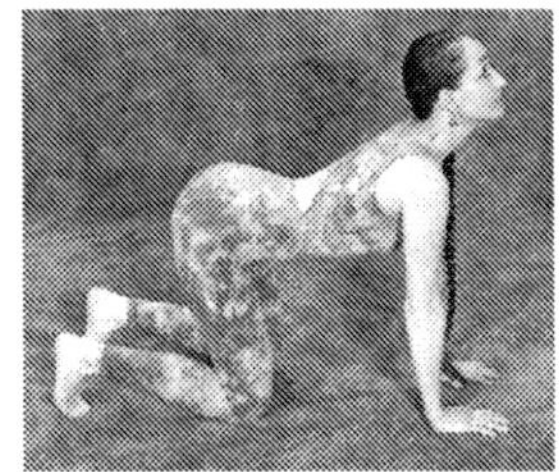
Fig. 21

Exhale, round your back as you pull your abdominal muscles up and in toward your spine. Reach your chin toward your chest. (Fig. 22)

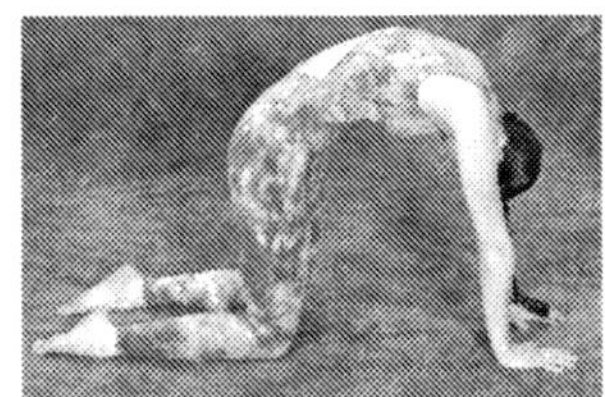
Fig. 22

Fig. 23

Fresh Air For Your Legs: Lie flat on your back. Slide one heel toward your hip, bending that knee. Inhale and raise the straight leg as high as your hip will allow and lift the same arm toward your leg. Exhale and lower the arm and leg in symphony with your breath. Repeat five more times on the same leg before changing sides. (Fig. 23) Variation: Raise the opposite arm and leg.

Standing Mountain: Stand with feet parallel. Inhale and raise both arms overhead. Hold this position for up to one minute. Exhale as you lower both arms to your sides. (Fig. 24)

Fig. 24

Fig. 25

Supported Tree Pose: With one hand on the back of a chair, inhale and raise one knee, sliding the sole of the foot up the inside of the other leg. Stop where you feel safe and check that your raised knee is turned out. Exhale slowly and remove your hand from the chair. Place both hands on hips and balance for up to one minute. Repeat on the other side. (Fig. 25)

Fig. 26

Solar Breath: Stand with feet parallel. Inhale and raise both arms overhead to touch fingertips. (Fig. 26) Exhale and bend forward from the hips to touch fingertips together either in front of your knees or shins. (Fig. 27)

Fig. 27

Keep your back as long and flat as possible when lifting back up. Repeat five more times, synchronizing breath with movement.

Fig. 28

Supported Triangle Pose: Stand with both hands on the back of a chair. Separate your feet as far as you can without sliding. Turn the toes of both feet to the right. Exhale and shift your left hip to the left while bending to the right out over your right leg. Hold here and breathe with the abdominal muscles five times. (Fig. 28) Inhale and return to standing. Exhale and change the direction of your toes to point to the left. Inhale. Exhale and shift your hip to the right while bending over the left leg. Hold for five breaths. Return to standing and walk your feet together.

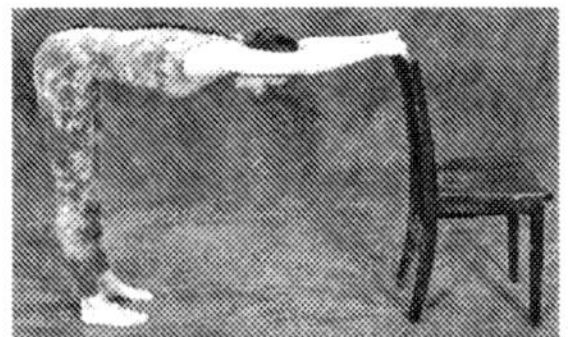

Fig. 29

Assisted Forward Bend: Inhale and lengthen your spine. Keep both hands on the back of the chair as you exhale and walk your feet backwards away from the chair as far as you can. Bend sharply from the hips and try to flatten your back like a tabletop. Position your feet parallel and hip distance apart. (Fig. 29) Hold here for five breaths. Inhale and walk back to the chair.

Fig. 30

Easy Spinal Twist: Sit in the chair with both feet parallel and flat on the floor. Inhale and lengthen the spine upwards. Exhale and turn gently from the waist to your right, grasping the chair arm and back with your hands. (Fig. 30) Hold this position for five breaths. Inhale and slowly return to face the front. Be sure to keep your spine lengthened for this exercise. Repeat on the other side.

Sitting Spinal Lift: Sit on the floor with both legs stretched out in front of you. Inhale and press both palms into the floor beside your hips effectively lifting your seat just barely off the floor. Hold for up to five breaths. (Fig. 31) Relax, and then repeat.

Fig. 31

Fig. 32

Bent Knee Forward Stretch: Sitting on the floor, bend one knee up and drop it to the floor so that the sole of your foot is against your inner thigh. Inhale and lengthen your spine then exhale and bend forward from your hips over the extended leg. (Fig. 32) Hold here for up to five breaths. Inhale and return to sitting. Repeat on the other side.

Legs Up The Wall: Lie on your back, hips against the baseboard and stretch both legs straight up the wall. Relax your arms to your sides. (Fig. 33) Breathe abdominally for five minutes. Fold both knees into your chest and hold for twenty seconds before inhaling and sitting up slowly.

Fig. 33

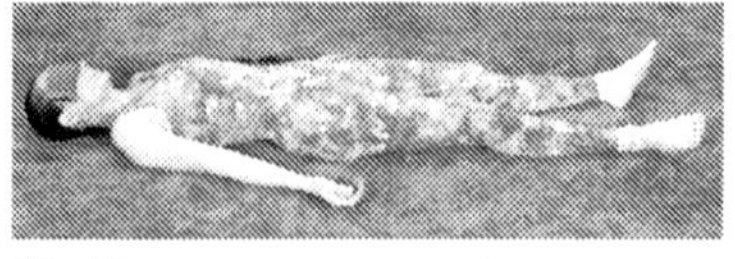
Fig. 34

"Corpse": Lie down on a firm surface with whatever pillow or blanket support you need under your neck, lower back, and knees. Close your eyes and breathe slowly through your nostrils for up to ten minutes. (Fig. 34)

WRITER WELLNESS CORNERSTONES

* Always start with relaxation and focusing your mind on your practice.

* Stretch large muscle groups first like your back and legs. Follow this with specific exercises for small muscle groups like shoulders, abdominal muscles and calves.

* Always coordinate breath with movement.

* Hold each pose for at least twenty seconds. Work up to holding some poses for one minute.

RELAX

The Benefits of Relaxation

Thirty years ago the world of science didn't acknowledge the benefits of a regular practice of relaxation or meditation. Never mind that thousands of individuals had conquered stress, hypertension and insomnia for thousands of years using the time honored wisdom of deep breathing coupled with visualization.

However, in reaction to the rising instances of stress-related illness, a series of controlled studies in the '70s by Dr. Herbert Benson at Harvard's Thorndike Memorial Laboratory and the Beth Israel Hospital in Boston resulted in the academic world's official recognition of the "relaxation response" in humans. Dr. Benson coined the phrase in his 1975 book about the study called *The Relaxation Response*.

Basically, they clipped some yogis up to some recording equipment while they meditated and found that the increased production of alpha waves in the brain, reduced oxygen use, decreased heart and respiratory rates and lack of muscle tension was a procedure accessible to these individuals at will. In other words, they could create the relaxation response whenever they wanted just by deep, controlled breathing and mental focus.

Dr. Benson concludes his initial study by saying, "...the Relaxation Response is a natural gift that anyone can turn on and use. By bridging the traditional gaps between psychology, physiology, medicine, and history, we have established that the Relaxation Response is an innate mechanism within us."

The health benefits of this innate human process include lower blood pressure and cholesterol levels, better use of oxygen and proper state of balance throughout the body and brain.

Books, videos, and classes abound on the subject of meditation and relaxation. If you have some aversion to the word "meditation" for whatever reason, just stick to "relaxation". The process is very simple and very effective, but must be adhered to on a regular basis. Daily for ten to twenty minutes for the rest of your life will prolong your life, boost your creativity and most importantly, give you a new tool for dealing with stress. The trick is patience.

According to Dr. Benson, four elements must be present in order to successfully call upon your own relaxation response. These are:

* A quiet place.

* A simple word or image to think about.

* A commitment to remain calm and not become involved in distracting thoughts as they occur.

* A comfortable sitting position.

A SIMPLE RELAXATION EXERCISE. Sit comfortably in a chair or on the floor. If you lie down you'll probably fall asleep and that isn't the goal. Conscious resting of the body and mind with stillness are your objectives. Tell yourself that you are not going to fidget for five minutes. Set a timer if you have to, but taking fifty to sixty breaths in and out constitutes about five minutes.

Take one to three deep cleansing breaths and relax your body from toe to head. Close your eyes. Concentrate on aligning the vertebra of your spine to allow as "clear" a passage as possible for your breath.

Breathe in and out normally until you find a steady, relaxed state. If you keep your spine positioned correctly, your abdomen will begin to flow out and in with each breath. Take ten breaths to become conscious of this procedure.

With each breath in, simply repeat "breath in" to yourself. With each breath out, simply repeat "breath out."

Basically, inhale and expand your abdomen, exhale and pull the abdomen muscles inward toward your spine. Repeat this controlled abdominal breathing exercise ten more times.

While you've been focusing on the breath and the body, hopefully your mind hasn't interrupted you with other things like the errand list, dinner menu, or the laundry pile. If so, consciously apply your attention to repeating "breath in, breath out," and pleasantly pack each distraction into a shoebox and quickly dissolve it with a splash of rainbow-colored fairy dust.

The key is patience and time. Set aside five minutes once or twice a day and work up to twenty minutes once or twice a day. It will take several weeks for you to notice how relaxation has become a part of your life and your day.

Knowing how to trigger the relaxation response expands your life and your choices. You have options available to you that other people don't because they don't activate them. By reminding your body and mind that calmness is a viable choice, you can live a more peaceful existence. Besides, slugging the bag boy who just threw a two-liter bottle on top of your French bread isn't worth it. Calmly take the bag to customer service, silently unload it on the counter and tell the manager you want French bread, not pita.

WRITER WELLNESS CORNERSTONES

* Health benefits gained from regular relaxation/meditation include lower blood pressure, increased oxygen absorption in the blood stream, better sleep and a state of balance throughout the mind-body spectrum.

* The relaxation response is available to anyone at will. Most people need "training" to remind them how to access the response.

* Knowing how to trigger the relaxation response expands your choices in life, thereby creating a more peaceful existence.

The Benefits of Relaxation Exercises

JOURNAL

Write about your family's methods for relaxing. While you were growing up, did your parents take the family on regular vacations? Do you schedule vacations from work on a regular basis? Do you ever use vacations to catch up on work or projects? Then it's not a vacation. Examine your history of taking a vacation. Do you need a new definition of what it means to take a break?

EXERCISE

Yes, I encourage exercise vacations as well as vacations from exercise. Depending on your fitness schedule and how disciplined you've been, you could reward yourself with a day or two without structured exercise. But if you haven't been very faithful, include moderate exercise every day of your time-out from work.

RELAX

Take a "mental vacation" by using one of your regular relaxation practices (you should have a regular schedule by now) to visualize a wonderful, stress-free spot where you can breathe easily and enjoy your surroundings. You don't have to create this place. It already exists in your subconscious. You just have to be open to discovering it.

Simply calm your body and mind with ten deep breaths counting backwards from ten in your mind, one count for every breath. When you have reached the number one, ask yourself to *picture* a quiet, peaceful, safe place for you to sit. Then breathe softly and wait.

A scene will gradually emerge in your mind. Don't interfere or add any details. The more relaxed you stay, the more intricate a setting your mind will present you. Keep breathing and watching the picture develop. When you feel yourself a part of the scene, take a snapshot. Commit every detail, direction and nuance to memory. Describe what you see. This is your private, unique tranquility space. You may add details and ideas now or at any time as if decorating a new living room with rugs and throw pillows. Take your time.

When you have engraved this place into your brain, count from one to five, opening your eyes on the count of five. With regular practice, you will be able to call up this scene of serenity at will.

NUTRITION

If you vacated your house and office of foods you should not eat, what would be left, and what would you throw out?

If you know your blood type, read and follow the plan in *Eat Right For Your Type* by Dr. Peter J. D'Adamo. Some blood types are easier to feed than others, but it's a good place to learn a great deal of helpful information about the foods you should and shouldn't be eating.

You can also try an elimination diet that challenges foods just about everybody should reconsider eating. Choose something from the food list below. Don't eat it for five consecutive days. Check all food content labels to be sure you aren't eating something you are trying to avoid. Pay attention to your body's reactions while not ingesting the targeted food.

After the five days, reintroduce small portions and notice any reactions you might have.

Here's the list (taken from *Five Day Allergy Relief System by* Marshall Mandell, M.D. and Lynne Scanlon):

Wheat	potatoes	chicken
Corn	pork	lettuce
Coffee	oranges	soy products
Cane sugar	carrots	peanuts
Milk	tomatoes	green beans
Eggs	yeast	oats
Beef	apples	chocolate

Watch for indigestion, gas, headaches, nausea, sleepiness, and diarrhea as signs that something you ate didn't agree with you. Avoid that food but always find a substitute so your "emotional hunger" won't feel slighted.

CREATE

Sketch and color your tranquility space as discovered during the relaxation exercise above. No matter how crude your drawing skills, this will help you continue to visualize and build on the scene better and better any time you want.

CREATIVE-WHILE-YOU-WORK IDEAS

Relaxing at work sounds like an oxymoron for some of you, but it's more of an attitude than a specific activity. It actually begins at home and gurgles over your edges at work.

While it may sound simplistic, meditation or relaxing is not the easiest thing to do. There are many reasons why it's difficult (hectic lifestyle, type of work, personal difficulties, social pressures), but serenity isn't about finding blame, it's about seeking balance. The seek is a lifelong quest.

Devote some serious energy and time to finding out what meditation really is. There are tapes, Internet sources and books by the hundreds. Meditation is so basic a concept it boggles me that there is so much material about it, but this makes it accessible when you go hunting.

Choose a process that seems applicable to your ideals about what relaxing should be. This could result in taking a meditation class, reading several books, or just deep breathing along with a tape from the library. Spend real time on the weekends (up to twenty minutes each day) feeling the sensations of meditation. It isn't anything like a whack on the head.

Meditation realization is subtle and delicate, but richly scented like the airs of Hawaii. Some days the aroma is overpowering, and other days it's barely there, but you can sense it nonetheless. Carry the subtleties of meditation with you to work.

When quandary arises, take a long, slow breath and use the quietude to remind yourself of the choice you can make to address the situation with calmness and peace. You just do. That's all.

It's all a matter of believing and telling yourself that you are NOT your work. Your work is what you do. Disengage in a healthy sense and realize that you are separate from work and that's okay. It really is.

Resourses to try:

The Intimate Art of Meditation, Jack Kornfield.

Learn To Relax & Let Go, Miracle Meditations tapes.

Meditation For Beginners, Maritza, Gaiam.com.

Breathing: The Master Key to Self-Healing, Dr. Andrew Weil.

NUTRITION

Eating the Right Words

There aren't many books or resources in my collection about dieting. Ever since someone pointed out that the first three letters of the word "diet" spelled "die", I quit looking at my eating habits from the perspective of what not to eat and changed my view to "how much of the right things can I eat?"

Apparently, a lot of other people are moving in a healthier direction as well. More "dieters" are changing overall lifestyles instead of just changing food intake. According to the Calorie Control Council (*www.caloriecontrol.org*), thirty-seven percent of adults were "on a diet" in 1986. With the new information available about long-term lifestyle changes necessary to good health, the number dropped thirteen percent to twenty-four percent in 2000.

But that still doesn't gloss over the fact that the U.S. Surgeon General has recently declared obesity an epidemic in this country.

There are no easy or quick fixes to revise your food intake. It's an individualized process of educating yourself to what works for you.

Here's what I recommend:

1. Keep a "Food and Feelings" journal. Eat what you normally do for one week and keep a meticulous description of your physical and emotional responses.
2. Research nutritional books and articles that prescribe a healthy process of eating food. Avoid programs that deny your body the necessary

functions of ingesting, digesting and eliminating a well-rounded menu.

3. Get professional assistance. Schedule a visit with a nutritionist, homeopathic practitioner, herbalist or a naturopath. They can assess your physical condition and will always listen closely to your personal health goals and incorporate them into their recommendations for you.

Keeping the "Food and Feelings" journal will help you and a healthcare professional you choose get a complete picture of what you eat and how it affects your life. It will also enable you to recognize the emotional aspects of eating.

Start with a clean sheet of paper folded lengthwise. Follow yourself through a typical seven days of normal eating. Down the left side of the page track what you eat and exactly what time of the day. Next to the food/liquids entries make notes about how you are feeling emotionally and physically. This is a catch-all column where you describe what's happening in your life moment to moment around the times you eat. It's important to write down how you feel BEFORE you eat and follow yourself physically for up to an hour after eating. Keep the format of this journal portable. A small stenographer's notebook with the division line already drawn for you is perfect.

Ask yourself these questions as you trace your food history for the week. Are you feeling energized an hour or so after eating or do you want to lay down and take a little nap? How do you feel after a stressful situation? Do you eat quickly or haphazardly in response to the stress? Do you feel nauseous or bloated soon after eating? Have you missed eating for several hours and are you feeling low on energy? Do you crave anything? When do the cravings occur in your day and how do you feel after giving in to the desire? When you are alone and eating, what do you eat and how much time do you devote to the meal? What is the difference when you are fueling up with other people involved? Do you eat better or worse? Do you ever overeat?

Use this journal to identify whether you are eating to live or literally living everyday just to see what and how much of it you can eat. With this history in hand, you can address to what level emotions are involved when you eat. The next step is researching and planning what will work the best for your lifestyle and personality.

Now that you've recorded your eating patterns, look at the right side of the paper and highlight the times you didn't feel your best. Shaking, cramps, and nausea can relate to emotional predispositions that your body is reacting to at the time you are also forcing it to respond to the physical demands of ingesting food. In other words, your body is already busy dealing with a stressful situation when you pile on food and draw its attention away from the stress. It has to switch gears from stress reduction to address the double cheeseburger, fries, and cheesecake you threw down your throat to ease the distress. Your body freaks and pays you back with an unexplained bout of diarrhea two hours later. You deserve it.

Learn to manipulate your emotions with deep breathing, visualization or meditation. Avoid screaming, greasy foods and medication. When you have relaxed, you can eat.

Expand your research to books, articles, and a trip to the nearest health food market. Seriously make the effort to increase your information base about what to eat and what nutritional supplements are best for you. You've already decided that you can't live like you are anymore, and while there are a multitude of practitioners out there with lots of advice, they can't hook you up to the Proper Diet Tubes and *make* you healthier. Only you can make the choices and follow through with a program that's right for you.

I already know it's a daunting task when you look at everything and every expert that's available. The following is my attempt to simplify the process for you. However, don't rely on only what I suggest as reference materials. PLEASE stretch your boundaries and work until you find the right nutrition plan for you. Here's my list:

Eat Right For Your Type, Dr. Peter J. D'Adamo, G.P. Putnam's Sons, New York, NY, 1996. When reviewed by several contemporary magazines this program gets bad ratings for being difficult to follow, but it works. (Web site: *www.dadamo.com*).

Prescription for Nutritional Healing, James F. Balch, M.D. and Phyllis A. Balch, C.N.C., Avery Publishing Group, Garden City Park, NY, 1997. This is a popular book that's easy to find and an all-inclusive resource that answers hundreds of issues surrounding nutrients, herbs, vitamins, and when to seek professional advice.

There are thousands of highly trained persons out in the world just waiting to give you their expert opinion about your best path to health and happiness. Realize that their words are simply advice you can choose to follow or not. It's your body, your life and your career. You should be in charge of what goes into it, on it and around it. But when the subject matter is something you need more information about, seeking the recommendations of experienced professionals is the best thing to do.

Besides the advice and referrals of your general health care provider, your community probably contains one or two complimentary health care individuals with a wide range of expertise, background and training. These include: homeopathic doctors, chiropractors, Chinese medicine masters, herbalists, ayurvedic doctors, naturopaths, osteopathic doctors, massage therapists and certified nutritional counselors. Look in the yellow pages of the phone book, ask friends, check the bulletin boards of health food stores and small cafes, the advertising sections of small press publications and the Internet to discover who is close enough for you to visit in person for a consultation.

Have your goals in mind or written down, take your "Food and Feelings" journal and talk honestly about your situation and your desires. Then LISTEN. If the practitioner doesn't offer to write his/her suggestions down for you, take notes. Ask what books she recommends on the subjects you've discussed. Go home and do what you can from the ideas and continue your research and experiments until you find the right balance for you.

Remember the changes your body undergoes daily. You will have to adapt your exercise and nutrition program as your body ages. Keeping track in your daily journal is a convenient way to notice when changes need to be made. It's also a great place to congratulate yourself on a regular basis about how well you're doing, feeling and creating as the result of an individualized routine of journal writing, exercise, relaxation, and nutrition.

WRITER WELLNESS CORNERSTONES

* Keep a "Food and Feelings" journal for a week to a month.
* Research nutritional programs to find the best one for you.

* Get professional help from a nutritionist, homeopathic doctor, herbalist, etc.

* Be prepared to adapt your food choices on a regular basis as you age, your health improves and your body changes.

CREATE

Make Wellness Happen in Your Life

"This is great, but how do I actually make this happen in my life?"

The answer to this question goes beyond basic self-motivation. Deep in the fibers of your muscles, burrowed in the core of your bones is the need to write. You know it's there because when you're writing, an inexplicable bliss surrounds you that serves as an energy source. It's where you draw your feelings of contentment, peace, and sensibility from when you are engaged in the process of creating your stories, articles, and poems. It's the magical power that drives artists of all makes and models to make it, do it, act it, write it, paint it or whatever until the project takes on a life of its own, serving the creator and the audience. You write because if you didn't, your body would explode from the sheer force of pent up creative urges. You write (or dance or paint or sing, etc.) or you die. At least it feels that way.

Incorporating a wellness lifestyle supports your longing to be creative. The first step is realizing and understanding the positive contribution healthy living can make to your creativity. The second step is alerting loved ones and pets of your desire to make the adaptations. The third step is a concrete plan of action that allows you to pretend for a while that you are a disciplined individual with a serious goal. The fourth step is accepting a new life plan and applauding loudly when your creative efforts skyrocket as you maintain a healthier body, mind, and spirit.

There are several models you can imagine to help see the supportive nature of healthy living to creative production. One is the vision of a set of scales. On one side your creativity; on the other side your health. The scales are perfectly balanced.

Another picture is a triangle something like the government's food pyramid that shows the basic building blocks of food necessary (in the USDA's opinion) to eat a balanced diet. Envision your creativity in the top most block of the pyramid with blocks below of nutrition, relaxation, exercise, journaling, etc., supporting your creativity.

Thirdly, is the shape of a pie with slices drawn in to represent the notion that all these parts contribute to your creativity and happiness.

Imagine a wheel with the center supported by spokes. In the middle is your novel, poem, or any creative project. Each spoke of the wheel contributes a different issue to help you build your creation.

Take a moment and sketch your own vision from one of the ideas above or something different to help your mind's eye retain an image of how all these issues build on one another to foundationally support your creative work. Post this sketch where you can see it every day.

Next, bring your family, friends and pets into the fold by explaining the changes. Nobody really craves change, least of all relatives. They like you in the slovenly mode. You are more easily manipulated in this mode. Those who resist your changes the most will be those who have had the most (real or imagined) control over your life. Beware of their doom and gloom comments about your plan. Ignore them.

Tell everyone you love him or her very much and that writing brings you true pleasure and that you want to devote more quality time to it. Ask them if they would be willing to help out with some of your plans and what they would be willing to do. Bring a specific list of items to this discussion. Don't go overboard. If you delegate all the household chores, pet responsibilities, childcare, laundry, car-pooling and food preparation to others, they will screw up their lips and look derisively at you and say, "And what are *you* going to do?"

Try one item per person and keep the rest of your chores for yourself. Make charts, lists, posters, and reminder lists, whatever it takes to help everyone, including you, stay on task. Give it a month. If none of the things you ask others to do gets done, reevaluate the plan and make another or hire professional help. If these options don't work, beg.

If you're limited on time and you want to get someone's attention, do things big. Preparing the New Life Schedule for your household should start with the biggest piece of paper or poster board you can find. But make a rough draft of your list on regular paper before copying it onto the billboard size version.

STEP 1: Clearly state your goal in writing and post it for everyone's benefit. "I want to finish my novel by November." Use whatever specifics such as dates and times you can expose yourself to. If you say, "I want to finish my novel at 10:00 p.m. on November 23," be prepared for the possibility that this won't happen exactly. But you have my permission to live dangerously. Be specific and see what magic transpires.

STEP 2: Chronicle every single moment of your life as you currently live it. Be detailed. Create a chart that shows where you are every half hour of the day. If you can't do this from memory, carry a blank chart (See Appendix B, page 162-163) around for a day or two and write in everything you do.

STEP 3: Circle or highlight the items from your standard day that can be delegated to other people. Make a list of the people who are cooperating with you and assign them the duties. Warning: BE SPECIFIC! Experience teaches that if you ask someone to "do the dishes" his or her definition of doing the dishes and your expectation may not be the same. "Wash, dry and put away all clean dishes everyday," will net better results. Or learn to live within other people's understanding of what it means to "do the dishes." To my newly married mother with a new baby and a dancing school to run, it meant throw the dishes away while your husband is at work. She bought a new box of Melmac dishes every week until he noticed they never ate off the same pattern for more than a few days.

STEP 4: Create a new schedule for yourself. This is the one you copy onto the large sheet of paper and post in the kitchen. Clearly mark the spaces of time set aside for your creativity.

STEP 5: Create a chore list that includes everyone and their agreed upon duties. List yourself to show the troops that you're right in there with them!

STEP 6: Evaluate. Designate a time period such as one month from the start of the new plan to gather and evaluate success. Be ready to listen to grumbling. Don't grumble back. Take a long, slow deep breath and say how happy you are with the progress you've made on your novel, and that if this keeps up you'll be done ahead of schedule! At least try!

If you're not a "schedule person," incorporating the changes and becoming more organized will be the biggest challenges to you. Look deep inside yourself to determine how important finishing your book really is. Maybe it isn't the priority you think it is. You've finished projects before—somehow—you can do it again. If not through the discipline of a schedule, then explain to everyone that you want these things done somewhere within the twelve hour space between nine in the morning and nine at night. Give everyone the same flexibility you need to finish the things that absolutely have to be done in a day. This equalizes the responsibilities and the consequences.

Some people are more accepting than others. The key to accepting life as it's doled out to you is patience. Acceptance is a coping tool, a learned response that enables you to understand that there is a reason for everything that happens. Regardless of your spiritual level, you are aware that no one person can comprehend the grandness of the scheme. It's just too large, but the outline does exist. The true variable is only that you have a choice. The choices you make when faced with any given situation determine what reason for living you experience next. To simplify it: This choice gets this, that choice gets that. There's a fundamental reason for the success of "choose a door and you get that prize" game shows. It's human nature.

Acceptance is NOT a sign of weakness or of giving in. It's one of the highest forms of creative responses a human being can utter. "It isn't what I had planned for, but this is what I've got, and I want to get there, so I'll use what I have to accomplish my goals." It's also an easier, less stressful way to live.

WRITER WELLNESS CORNERSTONES

* Incorporating a wellness lifestyle supports your longing to be creative.

* The first step is realizing the positive contribution healthy living can make to your creativity.

* The second step is alerting your loved ones to the changes you are making in your life to include wellness.

* The third step is a concrete plan of action involving everyone.

* The fourth step is accepting the new lifestyle for yourself.

If you were looking at a plot web for writing the Wellness way, it might look something like this (See Appendix C, page 164):

The fun part of constructing plot webs is seeing how far you can go, how many subordinate bubbles you can attach to every part of the web. It's also a very good exercise for the more linear of us who tend to require things in a neat and orderly list, and insist that no one goes on to the next thing on the list until the one before it is finished. I know, I know. My sister calls me anal retentive, too, but I like life sequential. But that will happen when they get ice cubes in Beelzebub's Bar and Grill.

The plot web image is a good way to see the big picture and to realize that all creativity happens in its own way, in its own time. Plot webbing your creative life will expand your vision of exactly what is involved in accomplishing your dreams. But how much is your dream worth to you?

All the schedules, exercise, plot webs and good intentions will not cover up the messier parts of the creative process that, sooner or later, everyone has to deal with. I'm talking about personal issues rather than spilled paint. There's guilt, fear, jealousy, and frustration, to name the top killers of the creative spirit. And don't forget ego, pride, and loneliness. There is also laziness, not enough money and criticism to deal with almost every step of the way. I haven't forgotten paranoia, divorce, or the big one, REJECTION. Having a story, book or poem turned down by a publishing factor is the single biggest reason more people don't write. Is your dream worth putting up with this and possibly more?

If your hope of publishing is valuable enough to bolster you against the incredible odds, then it's time you reviewed the material in this book and pulled your writing and wellness lives together.

You can start with this simple idea or design your own. The important thing is to work your way up to the big leagues of journaling, exercising, relaxing, eating right, and creating every single day of the rest of your life. Because the universe needs your energetic contribution if it's going to perpetuate itself and support us in our faithful attempts to be more like it—a constant celebration of the spirit of making something new in and with our lives forever. Like director Steven Soderbergh said when he won the 2001 Academy Award for directing, "Thank you to everyone who spends even a part of their day creating something, whether it be music, a book, a painting, or a dance."

The universe thanks you for being creative.

SCHEDULING. Until the Writer Wellness concepts become a natural part of your life, you'll probably have to follow some type of plan. The first step is intense scrutiny of your current life calendar.

You can use the chart provided in this book or design your own. If you create your own, I highly recommend doing this in a large, poster-banner kind of way to insure that you have your own attention. Others will note your seriousness as well. It's a fantastic exercise in time management and a true test of your dedication to accomplishing your creative goals. Stop here if you are only fooling yourself...

I thought so. Follow me, please.

You will need two blank copies of a Weekly Block Chart (see Appendix B, page 162-163).

DELEGATE. Take the time to fill one calendar with your current schedule for a full week from 6:00 a.m. to 12:00 midnight. Don't leave any task or activity out. If you have to be it, do it, wait for it, or get it, write "it" down on your schedule. The quickest way to the most reliable, useful information is to write in everything you do for week as you do it.

Sit back and take in everything you do in a typical week. Now take a yellow highlighter and mark one thing per day that you could delegate to someone else. Let somebody else do the errands on Tuesday.

DOUBLE DUTY. Use a blue highlighter to designate activities that you can't escape but the time used can do double duty. For instance, the piano teacher's house is too far from yours to leave your child for the thirty-minute lesson and get errands done (which someone else could do for you!). Take your journal, affirmation cards, relaxation tapes, or current writing project with you and work while you wait. Find at least one time period per day that can serve this double duty.

CUT IT OUT. Use an orange highlighter to signal the things you are going to throw out of your days completely. Time on the phone, with the television, computer games, or swirling around the Internet are prime targets for moments you could make much better use of. Make sure you find one time period/activity per day to cut out and change to time spent on some aspect of wellness and creating.

REINVENT YOURSELF. Take the second blank copy of the weekly block calendar and write a new life for yourself. While you work, make a separate list of the chores and errands you are delegating to others. Even five minutes here and there will invigorate your days and allow you the time to make these important changes.

Follow this new schedule for as many days as possible the first new week and evaluate at the end of seven days. Warning: Delegates may take a while to get into your groove. Remember acceptance and balance are your new tools. Go with whatever happens and do your best to show yourself and everyone else how committed you are to the new plan. Above all, be adaptable to the highs and lows you will undoubtedly experience as you grow.

A Day in Joy's Wellness Way

This is an example of many days from my history. As a result of my personal work at learning to be more adaptable and accepting, things change constantly. I still find time to journal, exercise, relax, eat, and work on my creative projects almost daily.

I get up when I want to, somewhere between 8:00 a.m. and 11:30 a.m. I drink a glass of cool water and one cup of decaffeinated chicory and barley pseudo coffee that is better for me than real java.

I unlock the room and the file cabinet and take out my current journal. I write three pages, single-spaced longhand with a black ink cartridge pen. I lock up the journal. Then I have to eat. I've been awake about one hour.

Brunch is light because I'll be eating again in two and a half hours. This meal can be turkey salad on spelt toast, a homemade spelt roll with real butter, spelt pasta salad or a small serving of cottage cheese with chicken strips. I eat a scrambled egg once a week whether I want to or not. After eating I take most of my supplements and a multiple vitamin.

Now it's time to shower and get dressed. Household chores, lunch for my children (they're home schooled, remember?), telephone calls and paying bills is squeezed into the middle of the day. This is my only opportunity to prepare dinner for that evening. I cook or bake whatever I can prepare ahead of time while the girls are having lunch.

I put the children back to their schoolwork and go to the computer where I check e-mail briefly and bring up whatever writing project I feel most excited about. I can usually choose from a new poem, romance novel, magazine article, query to an editor, or one of my nonfiction titles in progress. Once a month, it's the newsletter for our family dance studio of which I'm the editor. I set a timer and work.

Next, I check the girls' schoolwork and sit down to plan my studio class for that night. I teach one class, four nights a week. I eat a high protein food and drink a large glass of water. Here is where I take the rest of my supplements. After everyone is changed into the proper uniform for dancing or yoga or managing the front desk, we head to the studio, sometimes fitting in one errand on the way.

At the studio I prepare everything I need to teach a class that evening. I also have a light snack consisting of almond cheese, cooked turkey or chicken or soy crackers. I also take or return phone calls before my students arrive. After class, my spiritual partner, lover, and best friend in the world materializes and we exercise together or teach a yoga class or both. Then it's time to collect the younger daughter and head home. My mother brings the older daughter home after the studio closes for the evening. Both take classes almost every afternoon.

Dinner is hot in the Crockpot or waiting in the refrigerator to be reheated, served, and eaten. People rest for an hour after eating. I drink a glass of water after dinner and a decaffeinated instant coffee mix.

I write, revise, or edit for one or two hours before soaking twenty-minutes in a lavender bath and getting into bed for the night. On weekends, I write for more hours, but with a break every hour to check in with the children or eat or prepare one large family meal for the day. One night a week I order pizza and we go out to dinner two nights a month.

My loved ones are the best and the most helpful family a writer could ever wish for, but they didn't start out that way. Today, however, I have consistent help with vacuuming, putting away the clean dishes, washing/drying/putting away the laundry, walking the dog, feeding the dog and cats, brushing the dog, bringing in the mail, bringing in the newspaper, picking up five item grocery lists, dusting, paying the bills, picking up the clutter, teaching my classes at the studio, reading rough drafts, taking out the trash, bringing the laundry to the washroom, and changing the cat litter.

Granted, it doesn't all get done every day, but I've learned a new brand of acceptance and it allows me to write and write and write. The hardest part was teaching my kids the mantra, "Unless your hair or the house is on fire, do not scream, fight, hit, run, or knock on the office door. I love you."

WRITER WELLNESS CORNERSTONES

* Plot webbing your creative life will expand your vision of exactly what it takes to accomplish your dreams.

* There are messy parts to the creative process like fear, rejection, and procrastination. Depending on your dedication, you may or may not survive the odds. Having a wellness lifestyle plan in place can help you overcome some obstacles.

* The universe thanks you for being creative.

PREPARATION. If Writer Wellness is going to liberate your writing, you'll need to lay out a plan and stick to it. Everything you've read, written, or created thus far is part of the support system you'll use to restructure your life so you can write and live better. While trying things on for size for one week might be more to your liking, a 30-day trial run would better demonstrate the benefits and the possibilities to you and your circle of family and friends.

Begin by reviewing your writing goals. Take out the colored goal shapes and set them out in front of you on a flat surface. Get your journal and spend some time writing and illustrating some fantasies about your goals. For example, if one of your goals is to publish your novel, write about the incredible six-figure advance you receive from the publisher and the publicity surrounding this. Go extreme and go out on a limb as far as you want in depicting the amazing possibilities associated with your goals.

Now settle down to reality.

Pragmatism comes naturally to me, so imagining the potentials of my goals is always the challenge, but it thrusts me into a relaxed dimension that allows me to appreciate the unlimited potential of virtually everything and everybody in the universe. And it's fun. However, the phone company has yet to accept my creative ideas in exchange for payment of my telephone bill. Imagine my shock when the customer service representative told me that bartering yoga classes for my phone bill wouldn't fly with her supervisor. I had to get realistic and find the cash to make the grade.

In other words, start with idealism in all its glory and work your way to practicality by setting boundaries for yourself. Even if whimsy is where you spend most of your time, start dreamy, then get down to earth if you seriously want to live your dreams.

Ouch, that sounds like working *inside* the box, but it is actually working within a set of perimeters that make sense to your life as it is.

Your perimeter is discovered by a.) setting goals; b.) committing to those goals with unwavering persistence; c.) observing your current life and making the adjustments necessary to accomplish your goals; d.) enlisting supporters among family, friends, and hired help, and; e.) pledging every fiber of your being to following the program until your goals are realized.

I've broken down a 30-day Writer Wellness experiment into a check-list format and a day-to-day activity plan to make it easier to follow and stick to. You can photocopy the lists, but I'd rather you copied them in your own handwriting into a separate notebook with space for notes like encouragement, congratulations, complaining, and whining.

A. SET GOALS

How do you identify dreams and goals? You don't. They identify you. Dreams reoccur and goals follow you wherever you hide. They consistently seek and remind you of what you really want to be when you "grow up."

While reading a great novel, do you hear yourself saying, "I could do that?" When watching a well acted play, do you feel yourself in the actor's costume? No matter what obstacle is thrown into your path to being published, do you get over it and try again? These are the sensations to look for when deciding what your heart truly desires.

The reverse is also true. If that indescribable feeling isn't there and you find yourself easily distracted by other things, then you should look elsewhere for your heart's desires.

Your daily journal is the best place to discover the truth about goals. Talk to yourself in the pages and keep track of repetitive themes such as wishes for that big break in publishing. Be specific, but not rigid about how you envision the dream coming true. This helps the universe make it happen and enables you to recognize it when it does happen.

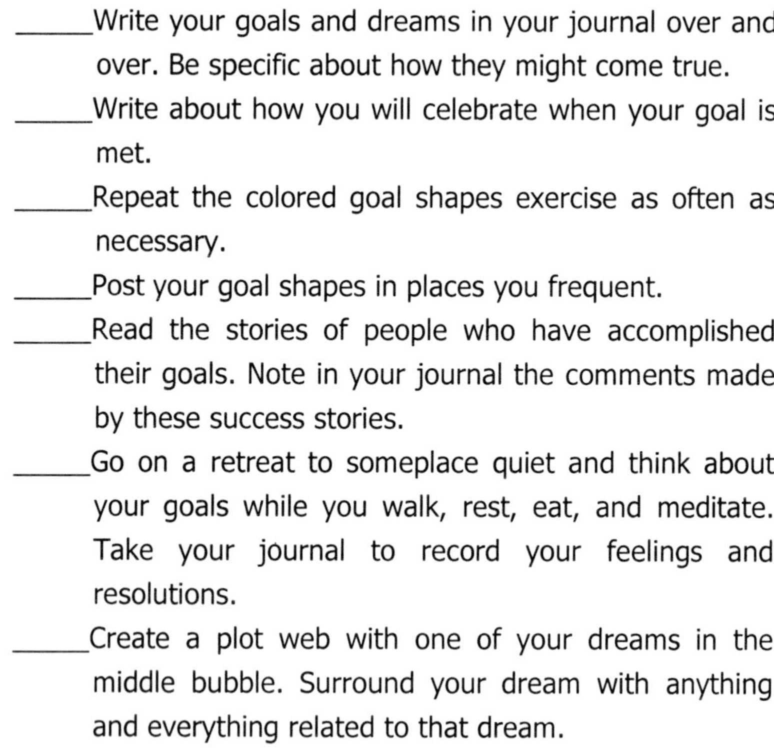

Set Goals Checklist:

_____Write your goals and dreams in your journal over and over. Be specific about how they might come true.

_____Write about how you will celebrate when your goal is met.

_____Repeat the colored goal shapes exercise as often as necessary.

_____Post your goal shapes in places you frequent.

_____Read the stories of people who have accomplished their goals. Note in your journal the comments made by these success stories.

_____Go on a retreat to someplace quiet and think about your goals while you walk, rest, eat, and meditate. Take your journal to record your feelings and resolutions.

_____Create a plot web with one of your dreams in the middle bubble. Surround your dream with anything and everything related to that dream.

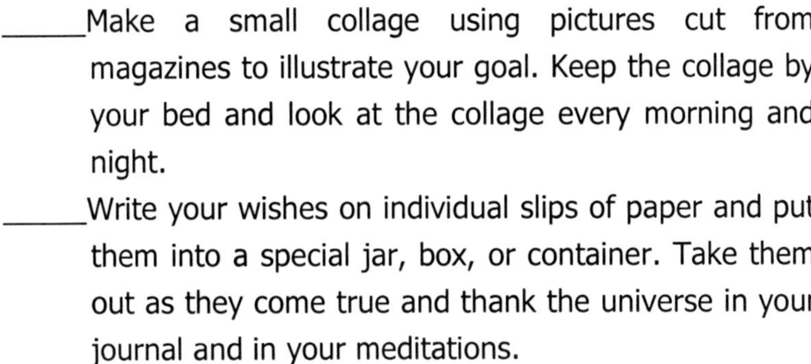

_____Make a small collage using pictures cut from magazines to illustrate your goal. Keep the collage by your bed and look at the collage every morning and night.

_____Write your wishes on individual slips of paper and put them into a special jar, box, or container. Take them out as they come true and thank the universe in your journal and in your meditations.

B. UNWAVERING PERSISTENCE

My mother still says, "It's not *what* you do, but *how* you do it." Sure, there are some new fangled contraptions for getting here and there, but the essential work is still the same. An airplane gets us there like a horse and cart used to. There are only so many "whats" to do, but an endless array of "how" to do them. Variety and choice have become a steady way of life in this progressive nation. It may be packaged differently, but everything, absolutely everything, answers the same basic human needs: food, clothing, shelter, and procreation.

Natural human ingenuity created variety, unwavering persistence is why we still create various ways to answer the basic needs. Dogmatic dedication is built into our genes. We keep going and going and going, and most of the time we don't even know why or notice that we just keep plodding along. It's because of our focus on survival. It's up to your heart to convince your head that accomplishing your goals is vital to your survival. After that, unwavering persistence in the direction of your dreams will be second nature. Working toward your goals will be "what you do" with your life.

Unwavering Persistence Checklist:

_____Make a detailed list of the activities necessary to meeting a goal. Break it down into small tasks (e.g., buy stamps, type query letter, stuff envelope, etc.).

_____Create a calendar with one activity from the list per day. Do it, check it off one day, one task at a time. Repeat this for every goal until it becomes second nature to you.

_____Keep a log of who, what, when, and where you send queries (or went to interviews, or submitted work, etc.). When the responses are received, note in the log what was said and the date you received it. Keep a separate log for each project.

_____Make brief daily journal entries about accomplishing each task.

_____Join a support organization (writers, artists, actors, etc.) to help keep you dedicated to your goals.

_____Report weekly to someone (loved one, relative, another artist, friend) about the activities you accomplished.

C. OBSERVE YOUR LIFE

To be metacognitive is to be intellectually self-observant of your learning *as you are learning.* It's a superior tool for mastering new skills quickly and efficiently. It isn't, however, an ability you can turn off and on at will. Metacognition is a sophisticated, learned skill that you teach your brain. Its purpose is to create a learning environment within your brain and body that enables you to perceive all educational experiences in a concise, consistent, and productive manner. By *observing yourself learn as you are learning*, you internalize new information much quicker and with greater ease. But it takes practice.

I first encountered metacognition in studies related to home schooling my daughters. As our educational methods are eclectic, so are our assessment procedures. The portfolio option is legally available in most states, which permits home-schooled children to present a collection of their school work from the year in place of taking a nationally normed, fill-in-the-bubbles, multiple choice standardized test.

The key to making a portfolio successful as an assessment tool is the self-evaluation process. Each month and each school year, my daughters review their work, choose activities representative of their development and write an explanation of what they learned, how it was learned and an opinion of their progress. I also write a lengthy narrative each month describing teaching methods, materials, advances or declines, and my opinion of the girls' improvements. At the end of the year, these progressive evaluations are a written record of their education.

After several years, this procedure has become habit for my girls as they witness and claim their learning. The question, "Am I learning anything?" isn't even part of the equation, because they constantly do quick retakes and are more secure about moving forward into new knowledge. This will eventually lead to the precious goal of being a lifelong learner.

For those of you who think this is a lot of writing, and when do we get any school work done, at the end of the year we are reviewed by a certified school teacher approved by the state board of education who is consistently amazed for ten years now that we always complete more work in a school term than most public school children or other home-educated students. We are a house of writers, one and all, so writing about how we learn has served our purposes immensely. It's also how you will learn to succinctly observe your own life to find the places you need to improve, clean up, or turn over to hired help.

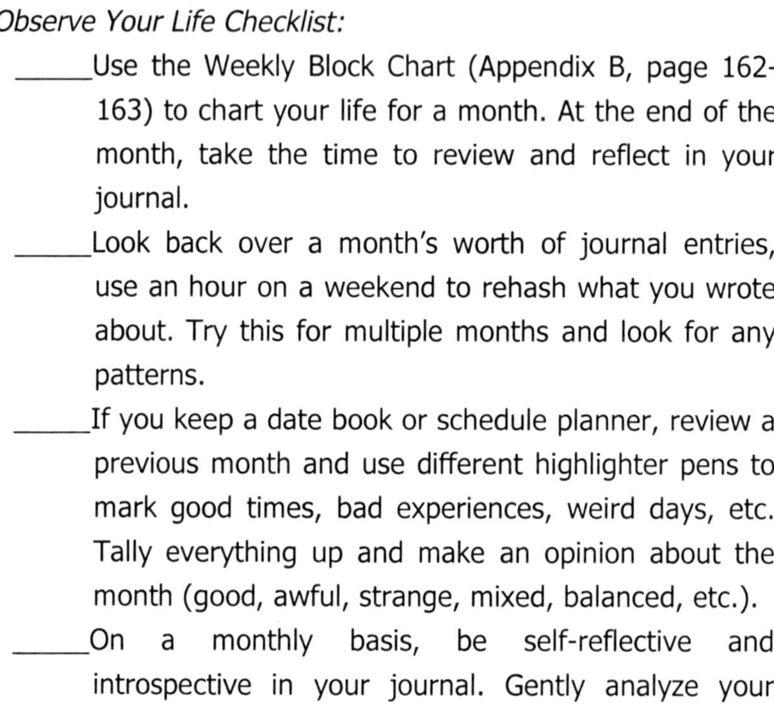

Observe Your Life Checklist:

- _____Use the Weekly Block Chart (Appendix B, page 162-163) to chart your life for a month. At the end of the month, take the time to review and reflect in your journal.
- _____Look back over a month's worth of journal entries, use an hour on a weekend to rehash what you wrote about. Try this for multiple months and look for any patterns.
- _____If you keep a date book or schedule planner, review a previous month and use different highlighter pens to mark good times, bad experiences, weird days, etc. Tally everything up and make an opinion about the month (good, awful, strange, mixed, balanced, etc.).
- _____On a monthly basis, be self-reflective and introspective in your journal. Gently analyze your thoughts and emotions.

D. MAKE PERSONAL CHANGES

Some people get violently ill at the thought of something changing. Being a creature of habit is safe and comfortable, but essentially unproductive and emotionally dissatisfying. I've learned that change is good, change is growth, and change is challenging. Change is everything you've taken pains to avoid in your life? What life? You probably like things where and the way they are. It's easy if life doesn't have to adapt. Maintaining the status quo is the safe life, but a life without impulse or drive. Granted, you have the freedom to choose not to change anything that might catapult your artistic career, but marking time in the same place eventually wears a rut in the ground.

Change is the only thing in life that is constant.

Change is integral to the evolution of any project, be it human, artistic, or universal. Some people think change means having to admit some kind of failure, that something didn't work, that's why it has to be changed. It's better to envision change as a metamorphosis, as a necessary tool supporting the birth of new ideas. Even then, the idea of change brings many to cussing, riots, and plotting. Definitely not the best atmosphere for new growth.

Fear is a very crafty motivator, and it plays a major part in someone's willingness to change. You have made that leap of faith and decided to set the goals, be persistent, observe your life, make the changes, enlist help, and pledge to your new life as a healthy, creative human, but the crowd surrounding you is used to the old you.

When they sniff change in the air, look out. Like animals running from a forest fire, don't get in their way. Try to be understanding. Take a breath and say to yourself, "Compassion," when someone starts ranting about how you can't change this or that. You've already made the personal adjustments without consulting them. You shouldn't have to clear it with everybody else before you rearrange your life to accommodate a healthier, happier, more creative lifestyle.

Part of the new plan involves enlisting the aid of others so you can journal and exercise a little bit each day. Don't alienate those whose help you will definitely need if you're going to succeed.

A woman named Lisa Alther put it best: "That's the risk you take if you change: that people you've been involved with won't like the new you. But other people who do will come along." (Taken from *Treasury of Women's Quotations* by Carolyn Warner.) It actually happens just as Lisa says. Others will come along. Don't be afraid. The best thing about the new people is that they don't have the old expectations of you.

In my opinion, it's really kind of goofy to sit in the same place. The fact that you've read this far is proof that you are part of the truly creative breed among us who survive on the human penchant for change.

Notice I've haven't been campaigning for you to change others, but for you to change *yourself.* Trying to change others *is* the cause of major wars. Be an example to the most stubborn members of your circle of life, and create happiness in your heart with the changes you make. This alone will bring the doubters along...eventually.

Life changes. Embrace it.

Make Personal Changes Checklist:

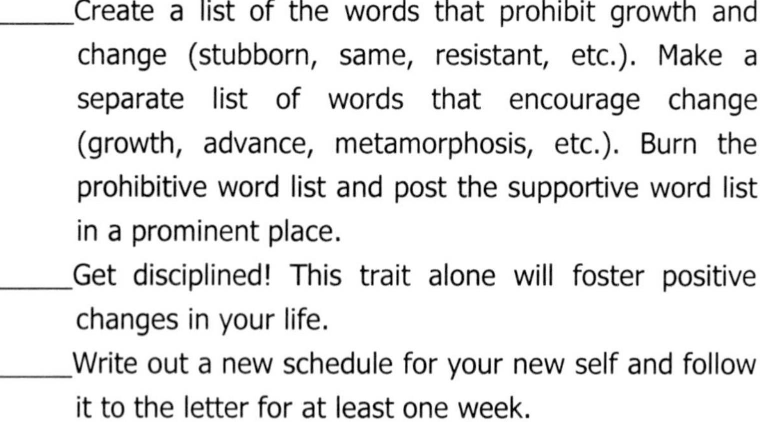

_____Create a list of the words that prohibit growth and change (stubborn, same, resistant, etc.). Make a separate list of words that encourage change (growth, advance, metamorphosis, etc.). Burn the prohibitive word list and post the supportive word list in a prominent place.

_____Get disciplined! This trait alone will foster positive changes in your life.

_____Write out a new schedule for your new self and follow it to the letter for at least one week.

_____Lie quietly with your eyes closed in a still, dark room and visualize your creative desires. Breathe slowly and softly as you carefully construct a picture of what your success looks like. Repeat this nightly before falling asleep until the dream is your reality.

E. ENLIST SUPPORT

When you need the house painted or you have to replace a secretary at work, you probably put an advertisement in the help wanted section of the newspaper. After some phone calls and interviews, you welcome the new worker into your world and hope they'll do a good job. Unless they paint the house orange or lose twenty clients with bad phone etiquette, you try to keep them around, if for no other reason than you need the help.

It's the same way at home. Or is it? Depending on the ages and pecking order of those you live with, some will be more willing than others to assume additional duties so you can journal, work on your novel, exercise, or whatever. Others will not be as cooperative. You can probably already identify the resistant and the supportive ones right off the bat. Here are a few suggestions from my family and household. Some worked better than others.

Enlist Support Checklist:

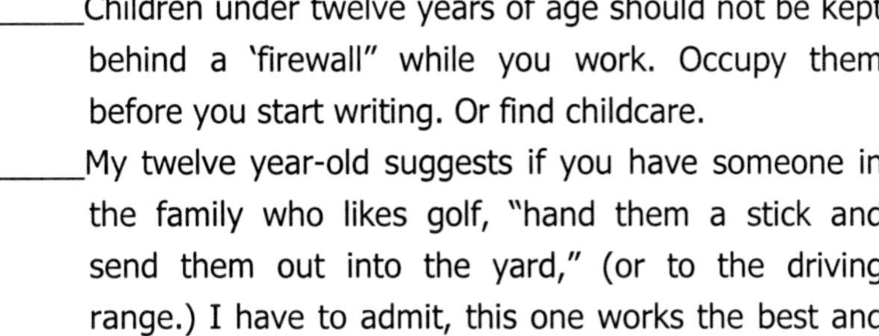

_____Children under twelve years of age should not be kept behind a 'firewall" while you work. Occupy them before you start writing. Or find childcare.

_____My twelve year-old suggests if you have someone in the family who likes golf, "hand them a stick and send them out into the yard," (or to the driving range.) I have to admit, this one works the best and

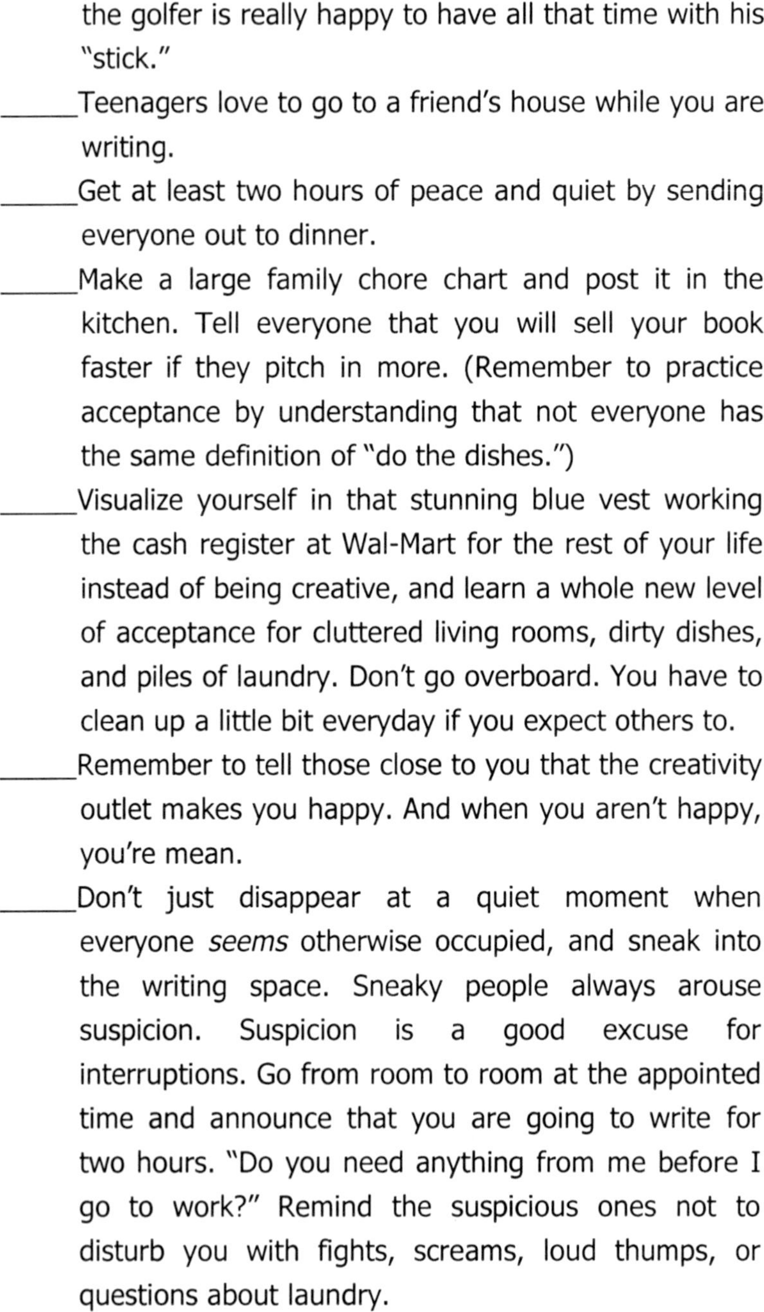

the golfer is really happy to have all that time with his "stick."

_____Teenagers love to go to a friend's house while you are writing.

_____Get at least two hours of peace and quiet by sending everyone out to dinner.

_____Make a large family chore chart and post it in the kitchen. Tell everyone that you will sell your book faster if they pitch in more. (Remember to practice acceptance by understanding that not everyone has the same definition of "do the dishes.")

_____Visualize yourself in that stunning blue vest working the cash register at Wal-Mart for the rest of your life instead of being creative, and learn a whole new level of acceptance for cluttered living rooms, dirty dishes, and piles of laundry. Don't go overboard. You have to clean up a little bit everyday if you expect others to.

_____Remember to tell those close to you that the creativity outlet makes you happy. And when you aren't happy, you're mean.

_____Don't just disappear at a quiet moment when everyone *seems* otherwise occupied, and sneak into the writing space. Sneaky people always arouse suspicion. Suspicion is a good excuse for interruptions. Go from room to room at the appointed time and announce that you are going to write for two hours. "Do you need anything from me before I go to work?" Remind the suspicious ones not to disturb you with fights, screams, loud thumps, or questions about laundry.

_____Post the following sign on your office door: "Do not disturb unless it's bleeding or on fire. (Or for large bugs, maybe.) Love, Me."

F. PLEDGE ALLEGIANCE TO THE PLAN

At this point, you should have a creative goal, learned persistence, made critical decisions about your life, made some personal changes to support your plan, and rallied the troops to help out. The final promise is at hand. It's time to face the toughest resister and take the vows to commit to the new deal you've spent so much time and energy developing.

You have to sign a contract with your body, mind, and spirit that you will follow this through to the new beginning. That fresh start is the wide open world of publishing your book, plays, or poems. It's the gallery where you sell your work. It's your byline on articles in magazines and newspapers. It's a new home for your creativity with different rules and responsibilities.

The desire and the dreams are potent, but how strong is the bond between you and the goal? How committed are you to stepping out of the current comfort zone into a world you have only wispy wishes about?

If you've ever been chairperson for the car wash or bake sale, you've experienced the difficulty in getting volunteers to commit time and resources no matter how great the cause. Most people can be classified as "conditional volunteers." "What's in it for me?" is their main concern. No amount of arm-twisting, pleading, teasing, or threats will move a "conditional volunteer" off their point of self-interest until you make it worth their while to serve time for the good of the organization. The greater good is rarely someone's priority. Granted, I've worked with selfless soldiers who sacrifice time, health, family, and money to serve, but the numbers are few.

There has to be a *reward.* A reward signifies *success.* To be a success, a personal definition is in order.

At the risk of being confrontational, I'm proposing that there is no one single right definition of personal success. Like my attitude toward creativity in general, it's effort that counts high on the list of explaining success. As many people as there are defining success, there exists an equal number of definitions for success. Did I confuse you?

> *"The only people who never fail are those who never try."* — Ilka Chase
> (taken from *Treasury of Women's Quotations* by Carolyn Warner)

Right away, the concept of failure enters the equation. The opposite of success is failure, right? Not if a healthy appreciation for effort is an equal part of the question. Can someone be considered a success who tries and tries but never knows victory? Trying is how you discover a definition of personal success. Sheila T. (from workshop) had an uncle who used to tell her, "You haven't failed until you give up."

The effort factor makes the definition pretty easy to accomplish. For example, list five things you've done to promote your writing (or acting, or painting, etc.) in the last four weeks. It has to be real activity, not dreaming.

1.____
2.____
3.____
4.____
5.____

If you can complete this list, you've had a successful month as a writer. If you can't fill in the whole list, you need to ask yourself why and if your goal to be a writer is "serious."

> *"I hope I have convinced you—the only thing that separates successful people from the ones who aren't, is the willingness to work very, very hard."* — Helen Gurley Brown
>
> (Taken from *Treasury of Women's Quotations* by Carolyn Warner.)

Even the smallest of positive energy in the direction of your goal is important. That's the first lesson about success. Defining personal success is learned through a series of honest physical efforts that don't always result in the *big success,* but they contribute to the *overall* success. They aren't failures just because the *big success* didn't happen with every effort. They are healthy steps along the journey to understanding that success is really another word for self-respect.

Pledge Allegiance to the Plan Checklist:

_____Write a contract with yourself. List five things you will do in one month to promote your writing. Sign and date the contract. Seal the contract in an envelope, address it to yourself and put a stamp on it. Give the envelope to someone you trust and tell them to mail it to you on a particular date (in thirty days). Spend the month meeting your contractual obligations. When the contract arrives in your mail, paste it into your journal and write about meeting the obligations.

_____Devote some serious effort to defining success for yourself. Write the definition into your journal and onto a separate sheet of paper to carry around with you at all times.

SAMPLE TWENTY-EIGHT DAY PLAN

This sample twenty-eight day plan is written as if you begin on Monday. It can be adjusted to suit personal needs. Also, other exercises can be substituted in place of what is suggested. Create your own basic chart that lists the five important components of Writer Wellness for each day (journal, exercise, relax, nutrition, create). Check off what you accomplish and always make brief notes about how much time you spend per activity.

After experiencing the process, schedule time to work on your current creative projects (novel, poems, painting, etc.) Writing can substitute for journaling, but journal as much as possible for ninety days before making the substitution.

Days 1-5:

___Journal (5 minutes)

___Exercise (5 minute walk)

___Relax (15 minute deep breathing with eyes closed)

___Nutrition (eat raw vegetables at lunch and dinner, 5 minutes eating, 5 minutes preparation time)

___Create (10 minutes collecting items for "Presenting Me" poster, Page 6)

(45 minutes total per day)

Day 6:

___Journal (5 minutes)

___Exercise (5 minute walk)

___Relax (10 minute breath meditation, "Breath in, breath out.")

___Nutrition (eat a food you've never tried before, 5 min.)
___Create (assemble all items for "Presenting Me," 5 min.)
(30 minutes total for the day)

Day 7:
___Journal (15 min.)
___Exercise (no exercise today)
___Relax (5 min. breath meditation)
___Nutrition (eat another food you've never tried, 5 min.)
___Create (Spend 30 min. creating "Presenting Me" poster)
(60 minutes total for the day)

Days 8-12:
___Journal (10 min.)
___Exercise (Twisting Breath, slowly for 5 min.)
___Relax (5 min. breath meditation)
___Nutrition (chose new recipes from a cookbook, 5 min.)
___Create (choose 3 goals and make colored goal shapes, Page 11, 10 min.)
(35 minutes total per day)

Day 13:
___Journal (10 min.)
___Exercise (15 min. three yoga postures)
___Relax (5 min. deep breathing)
___Nutrition (30 min. cook a meal with one new recipe)
___Create (no exercise today)
(60 minutes total for the day)

Day 14:

___Journal (10 min.)

___Exercise (no exercise today)

___Relax (5 min. breath meditation)

___Nutrition (eat an all vegetable meal, 30 min.)

___Create (finish goal shapes and post them in prominent places, 15 min.)

(60 minutes total for the day)

Days 15-19:

___Journal (15 min.)

___Exercise (10 min. walk and one yoga pose)

___Relax (listen to soft music in the dark for 5 min.)

___Nutrition (take a multiple vitamin, drink lots of water, 1 min.)

___Create (copy "Creative People" list into your journal, 5 min.)

(36 minutes total each day.)

Day 20:

___Journal (15 min.)

___Exercise (no exercise today)

___Relax (listen to soft music, 5 min.)

___Nutrition (read *Eat Right For Your Type* by Dr. Peter D'Adamo, 30 min.)

___Create (make creative affirmation cards to carry around, 10 min.)

(60 minutes total for the day.)

Day 21:

___Journal (15 min.)

___Exercise (no exercise today)

___Relax (listen to soft music, 5 min.)

___Nutrition (read Dr. D'Adamo's book some more, 30 min.)

___Create (make more creative affirmation cards, 10 min.)

(60 minutes total for the day.)

Days 22-26:

___Journal (20 min.)

___Exercise (10 min. yoga poses)

___Relax (abdominal breath exercise, Page 92, 5 min.)

___Nutrition (continue vitamins and water, 5 min.)

___Create (1 min. review of five creative affirmation cards)

(41 min. total each day.)

Day 27:

___Journal (20 min.)

___Exercise (no exercise)

___Relax (5 min. breath meditation)

___Nutrition (eat all vegetables at a restaurant, 30 min.)

___Create (complete "trouble bubble" plot web exercise, Page 21, 5 min.)

(60 min. total for the day.)

Day 28:

___Journal (20 min. review of the month)

___Exercise (no exercise)

___Relax (5 min. abdominal breath exercise)

___Nutrition (eat another new food, 5 min.)

___Create (design and make a "Wish Box," put some wishes inside, 30 min.)
(60 min. total for the day.)

Time breakout per week looks like this:

Week One:

Journal-5 minutes per day
Exercise-5 minutes per day
Relax-10-15 minutes per day
Nutrition-5-10 minutes per day
Create-5-30 minutes per day

Week Two:

Journal-10 minutes per day
Exercise-5-15 minutes per day
Relax-5 minutes per day
Nutrition-5-30 minutes per day
Create-10-15 minutes per day

Week Three:

Journal-15 minutes per day
Exercise-10 minutes per day
Relax-5 minutes per day
Nutrition-1-30 minutes per day
Create-5-10 minutes per day

Week Four:

Journal-20 minutes per day
Exercise-10 minutes per day
Relax-5 minutes per day
Nutrition-5-30 minutes per day
Create-5-30 minutes per day

Twenty-One Steps to Writer Wellness

Here are even more ideas for adding to your wellness plan:

1. TRIPLE 'A' YOUR PAST: Acknowledge that you share the direction of your life with a great source of power and love. You are not alone as you live the choices you make each day. Allow that great source to help you with every decision. Get advice from your personal power on a regular basis. Accept the realities of your past and accept yesterday as completed. You are a new beginning each day. Acceptance of the past as a place where you learned some lessons to help you with today is a way to free yourself of unnecessary guilt. Appreciate simplicity and detail as the secret messengers of serenity.
2. READ: Reading can be a writer's best pal or worst enemy. Adopt a policy to learn from everything you read. Above all, don't read instead of write. Read for pleasure and knowledge but always be conscious of the time you spend reading. It's very important to good writing, but reading overload is a convenient way to avoid writing.
3. JOURNAL: Journal writing should be as ritualistic as brushing your teeth, and I hope you brush at least twice daily. You can journal

twice a day, but once a day for twenty minutes is usually enough to clear the "brain mush" so you can focus on your writing projects. Experimentation is the key to finding out how your journal habit will best support your creativity. Use your journal as the daily dumping ground for anything that's on your mind and afterwards your mind will not be distracted while you write.

4. EXERCISE: This is another regular habit you need to adopt. Your body requires consistent physical activity to stay healthy. Hatha yoga, swimming, stretching, walking, dancing, and light weights are examples of good low impact programs that will sustain your body's health and your mental well-being, which will positively influence your writing. If you feel better, your self-esteem is in high gear and you can write better. The keys are regular, moderate, and long term when exercising for overall health.
5. CREATE SPACE FOR YOURSELF: Whether you choose to follow a feng shui diagram or just rearrange all that clutter in your spare room, a safe, dependable writing place is a must. Look over your living space and adapt a corner, a table, a room or even a portable box, and seriously address your writing there. Hobby or full-time, your writing deserves the recognition of a special place.

6. NUTRITION: Eat healthy foods, drink all the water you can stand and flush your system of toxins regularly. A detox tea is usually the mildest way to go for this, but seek counsel from a homeopathic physician, naturopath, chiropractor or master herbalist. They can recommend nutrition paths for you, address your supplement needs and help you with detoxification. A regular full-body massage is excellent for ridding the body of waste and it's a heavenly experience.
7. RELAXATION: Deep breathing, meditation practice, guided visualization, relaxation tapes or just a twenty-minute nap with nothing on your mind contributes immensely to your overall health. This is a lifestyle adaptation, too, so it must be approached with patience. Begin by incorporating five minutes of deep breathing practice once or twice a day. Gradually, over many months, extend your relaxation period to twenty minutes. Take your time. Breathe in through your nose for a slow count of four, and then exhale through your nose for a slow count of four. Work up to 100 breaths. Every breath counts.
8. AROMATHERAPY: Wonderful scents make sense to your body's sense of composition and cooperation. The body and mind's reactions to scent stimuli are subtle, but consistent. Scented candles, fresh flowers, aromatic

essential oils and boiling dried herbs in water on the stove will elicit a response from your body depending on the scent. Diane Ackerman, author of *A Natural History of the Senses* says, "One of the real tests of writers, especially poets, is how they write about smells." This is because of the physical responses and the memories created by a particular smell. Try lavender for peacefulness, geranium for balance, or ginger for memory.

9. NETWORK: A poet friend asked me how another poet friend got his nomination for a Pushcart Prize when the first friend was more widely published. I answered, "He networks, you don't." Writing groups, conferences, classes, workshops and meetings with other writers can only help your work if you are able to stay detached while someone is commenting on it. By networking you can promote your work of course, but it's better to view networking as a learning opportunity. Writing style, voice, grammar and methods can all be gleaned from being actively involved in writer networking. Most workshops don't force participation. In fact, the really good ones are encouraging regardless of whether a writer reads work out loud. You can absorb a great deal about the biz just by listening. If you're worried about wasting your time around writers who ask questions you already know

the answers to, think about it as learning how you will answer these writers' questions when you are someday in front of a group of writers. Connect.

10. TIME: Making time to write is about finding balance in your life. Balance is derived from setting proper boundaries. How far away will you let guilt, other people's expectations and self-doubt drag you from your heart's desire? Complete a weekly chart that shows what you are doing every half hour from 6:00 a.m. to midnight. Develop a sense of priority about your writing and learn to delegate some of your chores and write instead. Enlist family and friends and professionals who will take over some of the laundry, errands, cleaning or cooking. A former Writer Wellness Workshop student filled out her weekly chart and immediately hired a housekeeper. She finished her book three months later after having worked on it for years. Tell everyone in your life how important your writing is to you and they'll eventually sign up to support you. People who say, "I don't have time to write," don't ever write because they're afraid of actually having to do it.
11. MAKE THE CHANGES: It's one thing to discover what you need and another thing to go after it. Once you plan out the lifestyle adaptations that will support your writing, you must make

the commitment to follow the planned course of changes. Wanting to write and reading about others who write and how they do it is a great start, but it won't get you published. You will reach your writing goals by devising a series of accomplishable mini-goals with planned rewards for yourself along the way. This bolsters your right brain's self-esteem. Honor your creativity in some way as often as you can.

12. SCHEDULE: After examining your weekly time chart, delegating and making the commitment, you need a definite schedule. You should at least set up a framework of when you will write and what, and try to stick to it. Some people thrive on schedules, others get physically ill at the thought of being on time for something. No matter which you are, outline a schedule in writing and set a deadline. Post it in the creating space and make a note each day about what you accomplished.
13. LISTS: Another option is to make a detailed list showing everything you will do to meet your goal. When it is done, check it off with a bright colored marker, celebrate and move on to the next thing on the list. It's one of many games you can play with your mind to reach a deadline.

14. BOOK LOOKING: All writers should be up to date on the publishing industry. Book looking is more than visiting the library. It is reading several pages of R.R. Bowker's *Books In Print* at least once a year, spending a long time looking at books in stores and reading current trends in the publishing industry publications. When you're in a certain section of a bookstore, listen to the people talking about books. Listen to the sales clerks and above all, ask questions about what's going on with publishing. Ask why a particular book is displayed the way it is or when the next author will be signing books in the store. The writer is the raw meat of the publishing process, like it or not. Publishers cook it on a high-heat grill until they think the public will buy it. Don't forget the reality shaking procedure of visiting yard sales and flea markets to see paperback novels at ten cents each.
15. PUBLISH: Be more open to the new technology of widely available publishing options. Don't downgrade the family newsletter you PUBLISH. Don't diminish the personal greeting cards you PUBLISH for family and friends. Be the first to expand your personal definition of being published to include anything you write and circulate. If you don't have any of these outlets, create them for yourself.

16. WRITE-WRITE-WRITE: This may seem like an obvious step that doesn't need mentioning, but too often writers forget that their work is like exercise to their muscles. Writing the good stuff takes a regular approach of writing not-so-good stuff. Journal entries, letters, essays, poetry, lists, notes, cards, and scripts count toward daily writing. Keeping a notebook with you all the time allows you access to the tools of pen and paper wherever and whenever you have the time. Take advantage of any opportunity to write.
17. TRAVEL: Taking a trip, short or long, is a healthy way to relax and develop perspective. Take writing tools with you, of course, and spend long hours viewing different places, people, activities and things, and writing about them.
18. HEALTHY HEARING: Since I was raised in a very musical home, I consider music an important part of my daily routine. I like the accompaniment in the background when I write, cook, teach, study, make love, dance, and think. Surround yourself with the type of music that contributes to what you're doing. The television doesn't count.
19. COUNSELING: To receive counsel is to get ideas from other people. Counseling is advice from your father, guidance from a professional, instruction from a teacher,

recommendations from friends, a warning from your spirit guides, or a friendly suggestion from your mentor. Networking, classes, conversations and appointments with professional counselors will enable you to trust your own judgment eventually. Learn to talk and to listen and to write about your questions, and the guidance you hear and feel inside your own heart and body will be your best advice.

20. ABSORB THE ARTS: Writing is historically known as "solitary confinement" to a desk, some kind of chair and the writing equipment of your choice. Writers, alone, sit or lie down and write their stories apart from the rest of the world. I'm doing that right now. Even the cats have gotten bored and left me. The creative process, however, thrives on a universal sense of empathy for the effort put forth. This cooperative appreciation of a creative work of art happens when others appreciate it. Expand your own appreciation of the work of other artists in any field by making more of an effort to attend concerts, ballets, galleries, theatres, etc. The respect you learn to give other creators will always come back to your own creative works.
21. LOVE: Practice more hugging and more smiling. Say, "I love you" out loud to your

family every day. Love truly is the reason we are here. Learn it. Live it. Share it.

WRITER WELLNESS CORNERSTONES

* Triple 'A' your past: acknowledge, accept, and appreciate.
* Read
* Journal
* Exercise
* Create space for yourself
* Eat healthy foods, drink water and take vitamins and supplements
* Relax or meditate on a daily basis
* Fill your world with wonderful scents
* Network within your artistic world
* Appropriate time from a perspective of balance in your life
* Plan and go after the changes you want to make in your life
* You need a definite schedule no matter how random you like to be
* Lists can sometimes help keep you on task
* Book-look, be up-to-date on the publishing industry
* Publish your writing in a variety of ways
* Write something every day
* Travel
* Include music
* Counseling can be a good listener
* Absorb the arts, take in other mediums and genres
* Love

Twenty-one Steps To Writer Wellness Exercises (* set a timer)

JOURNAL

Copy all twenty-one steps into your journal the first day. Choose one step per day over the next twenty-one days, copy a step a day and examine your feelings about that step. Make a plan a day in writing for accomplishing that step in your life. (* 15 minutes)

EXERCISE

Choose any form of exercise agreeable to you at this point (walking, yoga, exercise equipment, weight lifting, etc.) and workout for twenty-one minutes twenty-one days in a row. (* 21 minutes)

RELAX

Relax with deep breathing in a comfortable position, eyes closed for five minutes a day twenty-one days in a row. (* 5 minutes)

NUTRITION

Choose a food that you eat but know isn't healthful for you. Substitute something better for twenty-one days. For example: exchange potato chips for low-salt rice crackers or trade ice cream for flavored Italian ices. Pay attention to how many days you feel "insulted" by this change and when exactly you stop craving physically and then mentally the discarded food. Don't eat less of the new food. This will clue you in to how emotionally addicted you are to the negative food. The longer it takes for you to "feel" satisfied with the new food, the more emotional the attachment to the old food.

CREATE

Design and create goal charts for twenty-one days of journal writing, exercise, relaxation, and nutrition. Use positive reward stickers or a simple check mark to note successful days. Paste these charts into your journal once the twenty-one days are completed.

Follow this exercise with a contract written in your journal about which twenty-one steps you are going to incorporate into your new life.

This idea can be used to accomplish a special project such as a new chapter in your novel, a new collection of short poems or lyrics for a song you're working on. Make a twenty-one day chart and put a star on the days you achieve something toward the goal.

CREATIVE-WHILE-YOU-WORK IDEAS

Write each Step on an index card and take a different one to work with you for twenty-one consecutive days. Put the card someplace where you will see it often.

Do mini-exercise sessions of one to five minutes throughout the day. While waiting at the copier, do leg lifts or Standing Mountain. On bathroom breaks, complete ten Twisting Breaths before going back to your station. Keep a written tally of what and when you exercise until you have 15 minutes of exercise while at work a day.

You Can Take This Idea Anywhere!

Unlike your hide-under-the-bed exercise equipment, you can take the Writer Wellness program virtually anywhere you can take a normal travel suitcase. Hotel, campsite, or a relative's condo, it's easy to bring along your Wellness tools no matter how light you're packing.

Exercise: (10-15 min.) I may be going out on a limb here, but I'm assuming you'll be wearing shoes on your trip. Pack a quality pair of cross-trainers or walking shoes. You can even wear one pair of supportive tennis shoes the whole trip, just pack a set of sport insoles to add when you power walk around the hotel parking lot five or six times before the included-with-the-room breakfast buffet or just before dinner. One pair of shoes!

Including hatha yoga stretches is just as simple. If you've progressed enough to appreciate a yoga sticky mat (see resources at the back of this book), you can buy inexpensive, portable ones from many suppliers. It can stand up to incredible treatment and fits into a standard pack-and-roll type luggage or rolls up to slide into a backpack. Of course, they are sold with specially designed carrying bags. Ten minutes of yoga before your morning shower or evening bath and you haven't lost your groove just because you're on the road.

Journal: (10 min.) This one's easy. Pack a blank book or take along your regular journal notebook. When you are waiting somewhere on your trip, write. Sketch what you see, record snippets of overheard conversations, and jot down your thoughts. Keep it with you; don't check it inside of potentially European bound baggage when you're only headed to Cleveland. Nothing messes up a great trip like all your private journal entries visiting faraway ports-of-call without you. Shudder the thought. It also makes for interesting entries to journal on motel stationary and pasting the pages into your journal when you get home. Ten minutes is plenty. Save longer entries for when you get home.

Nutrition: (1 min.) Pack your supplements and vitamins in pillboxes or plastic baggies and toss them in with your toiletries. If you require any special foods, this takes a bit more preparation, but keeping to your food program while traveling is a lot less hassle than dealing with bloating, burping and gas just because you didn't want to carry along your bread. Learn to eat more cooked vegetables and all white meat (if you eat meat) when you travel, and drink lots and lots of water. That's a menu anybody can find away from home. I recommend packing at least one snack you are passionate about for when you're hungry and can't find anything on the midnight vending machine raid that won't upset your system.

Coming home from a trip where you've eaten the proper foods is more pleasant, too. No bloating, headaches, or toxic belches to deal with once you're back in your own pantry.

Relaxation: (5 min.) This takes practice, but it's the lightest item you'll be packing. It's your breath and the vivid images you've been practicing in your mind during all those daily relaxation sessions at home. Anywhere, anytime, for any reason, you can find a place to stand or sit still, close your eyes and count breaths. About 20 deep abdominal breaths should slow your stress meter down, but 50 would be better. Do this as often as you get the chance during the whole trip. Down time in your hotel room is better spent relaxing and meditating than checking out the rental movie menu on the television.

All together, that's less than thirty minutes per day spent on your Wellness regimen, but the total benefits will amaze you. During and after the journey you'll maintain awareness and a positive attitude that will support you throughout the trip.

WRITER WELLNESS CORNERSTONES

* The Writer Wellness program is very portable. It can go anywhere.

* Walking is an easy exercise to include with your travels.

* Yoga stretches are simple to do in a hotel room, exercise room, or poolside.

* Pack your supplements and special snacks. Drink lots of water.

* Relax/meditate for five minutes every day of your trip.

Writer Wellness Affirmations

Creative use of positive affirmations can be very helpful in your journey to better health and creativity as a writer. Below is a list that you can copy onto index cards and carry around with you, use as journal prompts on a regular basis, or as phrases to post in prominent places where you can reflect on them several times a day. If you've never tried positive affirmations and you aren't sure if they'll work, just read *The Little Engine That Could* again.

I am a brilliant, gifted writer.

I am a healthy person.

I am allowed to be healthy and creative.

I am willing to embrace the changes necessary to become a healthy writer.

I deserve a healthy, creative life.

I am willing to learn to be healthy.

I am willing to accept my new levels of health and creativity.

I begin every day by promising myself to be responsible for my health and well-being.

I am allowed to live a healthy, creative life.

I make productive nutrition choices that support my creativity and health.

I journal regularly to cleanse my mind and emotions.

I am dedicated to a lifestyle that supports my creativity in a healthy manner.

My health and creativity prosper through my dedication to healthy concepts and ideas.

My body is constantly changing and I adapt constantly.

My desires to be healthy and creative are worthwhile.

My creativity is strong and perpetual because of my healthy lifestyle.

I end every day by celebrating my health and creativity choices.

I have the discipline to maintain a healthy lifestyle in support of my creative desires.

I am confident in my choices for health.

I deserve five minutes a day to myself for relaxation or meditation.

I have all the tools I need to be healthy, calm and creative.

My healthy lifestyle and creative growth benefits me and those I love.

I trust my body and my mind to provide the guidance I need to live a healthy life.

I am willing to let go of negative habits that do not support my creativity.

I am connected to my inner wisdom and I am willing to listen to it.

I desire a healthful lifestyle that supports all my creative efforts.

I have all the ability I need to bring myself to a relaxed state of body and mind anytime I want or need.

I choose healthy living to support my wishes for a creative life.

I choose positive, supportive habits that encourage me physically, mentally, emotionally, and spiritually.

I trust the process to help me regain my health and to be more creative.

I accept that I must live in one moment at a time.

Writer Wellness Warriors

Practically everything is more enjoyable when shared with like minds. Here are some tips on starting your own pack of Writer Wellness Warriors.

Join writers' groups. Start a local writing club if there isn't one around you. Most states have statewide organizations and there are numerous national level associations devoted to writing craft and publication. Network within the group to find two or three other people who want to improve their creativity base through the Wellness program. It only takes two other writers to start your group.

If you have writing friends from the networking you did at a conference, include them via e-mail, telephone and letters. If none of those options are open to you, post a notice on the bulletin board of the libraries in your area inviting writers to join in a different kind of creativity support group that will enhance their professional and personal lives.

You aren't teaching them how to organize their lives around the Writer Wellness concept. Everyone is responsible for reading this book and developing his/her own plan. Meetings or correspondences are where members explain what's been working for them and what hasn't, giving tips to other members on how to find a yoga class, locate the health food store or what books the library has on journal writing. Maybe someone knows of Web sites that are supportive to a wellness program.

Members could meet once a week for a thirty-minute group walk around the park or in a mall (if you have a mall that allows exercise walkers).

Sharing recipes for low-calorie, high-energy snacks and foods is a great way to enjoy a picnic or dinner at someone's house.

Invite a yoga instructor to give you a 15-minute demonstration of postures and explain a relaxation exercise to everyone. Sign up for a yoga class as a group and schedule practice sessions together in between classes.

Have everyone bring in at least one book they own or have borrowed from the library about exercise, nutrition or writing. Compile a resource list, print and distribute to the members at the next meeting.

Set up an e-mail reminder system where members send notes to each other reminding them to journal, exercise, relax, and eat a good meal that day.

Have one member per month e-mail a daily affirmation to everyone to serve as a journal prompt. At the next meeting, members bring in their journals and read selected responses to the prompts. Assign a different member to send out the prompts the following month.

Discuss ideas for keeping personal journals secure in your homes and while traveling.

Expand meetings to include discussions about each writer's work. Consider reading written works created before embarking on the Writer Wellness warpath. Every three months writers read new projects or pieces of work and discuss how health and wellness are contributing to their creative process.

Visit a bookstore together.

Meet in coffee shops to journal together.

Have everyone bring journals to a regular meeting and respond to the same journal prompt from an affirmation book, set of runes, passage from a favorite book, a poem or quotation.

Rent exercise videos and watch them together.

Celebrate everyone's progress on a regular basis every three months. Be creative. Take "before and after" pictures and make a poster showing the group's support of each other.

Choose a book that relates to the issues of Writer Wellness and have a discussion of the book after everyone has read it.

Create an inexpensive "sharing letter" that everyone takes turns designing and printing on their home computers. Include recipes, member's contact information, planned events, suggested reading and details about someone's experience with an exercise or meditation class. Because a different member a month produces the "sharing letter," individual personalities and skills are highlighted.

The goal is mutual encouragement and self-education. You may have brought the group together, but the best leaders empower the followers.

And keep in touch with me. I really want to hear about your successes, big and small.

Joy Held, P.O. Box 1322, Parkersburg WV 26102-1322

E-mail: joybeth@wirefire.com

Web site: *www.writerwellness.com*

Joy is available for workshops and individual coaching.

Additional Resources

JOURNAL WRITING

Cameron, Julia. *The Artist's Way: A Spiritual Path to Higher Creativity.* Los Angeles: J.P. Tarcher, 1992.

Reeves, Judy. *A Writer's Book of Days.* Novato, California: New World Library, 1999.

EXERCISE

Miller, Elise Browning and Carol Blackman. *Life Is A Stretch.* St. Paul, MN: Llewellyn Publications, 1999.

Rush, Anne Kent. *The Modern Book of Yoga: Exercising Mind, Body and Spirit.* New York: Dell Publishing, 1996.

NUTRITION

Balch, James F., M.D. and Phyllis A. Balch, C.N.C. *Prescription for Nutritional Healing.* Garden City Park, NY: Avery Publishing Group, 1997.

D'Adamo, Peter J., M.D. *Eat Right For Your Type.* New York: G.P. Putnam's Sons, 1996.

RELAXATION

Budilovsky, Joan and Eve Adamson. *The Complete Idiot's Guide To Meditation.* New York: Alpha Books, 1999.

YOGA SUPPLIES

Hugger Mugger Yoga Products, 3937 South 500 West, Salt Lake City, Utah 84123, 1-800-473-4888, http://www.hugger mugger.com.

Appendices

APPENDIX A

"Things To Do When You Are Bored"

investigate the past
watch an insect
read a book
listen to a book on tape
draw
read poetry for 15 minutes
write a page of anything
conduct science experiments
research a dance topic
create a small museum
write letters
start a book discussion group
volunteer to do something
teach
choreograph a dance
write music
write a short play
garden
clean
read the newspaper
read a whole magazine cover to cover
play solitaire
go to the library
bake or cook
make a list of questions about anything
play a game

assist someone with a project
sew
knit
crochet
make a toy
make a time line of your life to date
take a walk
feed and water a pet
visit a restaurant or coffee shop
visit an historical reenactment
tape record yourself reading or singing or playing an instrument
make a home video
make a scrapbook about something you've done or like
plan a party
have a party
watch old classical movies
write in a journal
listen to foreign language tapes and learn one phrase
clean some more
make greeting cards
take pictures
exercise
play
lie in the grass and watch clouds, draw what you see
make a "Five Years From Now" plan
work with clay
make a collage from magazine clippings
build something
clean some more

APPENDIX B

Weekly Block Chart

TIME	MONDAY	TUESDAY	WEDNESDAY
9:00am			
9:30			
10:00			
10:30			
11:00			
11:30			
12:00			
12:30			
1:00			
1:30			
2:00			
2:30			
3:00			
3:30			
4:00			
4:30			
5:00			
5:30			
6:00			
6:30			
7:00			
7:30			
8:00			
8:30			
9:00			
9:30			
10:00pm			

Weekly Block Chart

THURSDAY	FRIDAY	SATURDAY	SUNDAY

APPENDIX C
PLOT WEB FOR WRITER WELLNESS

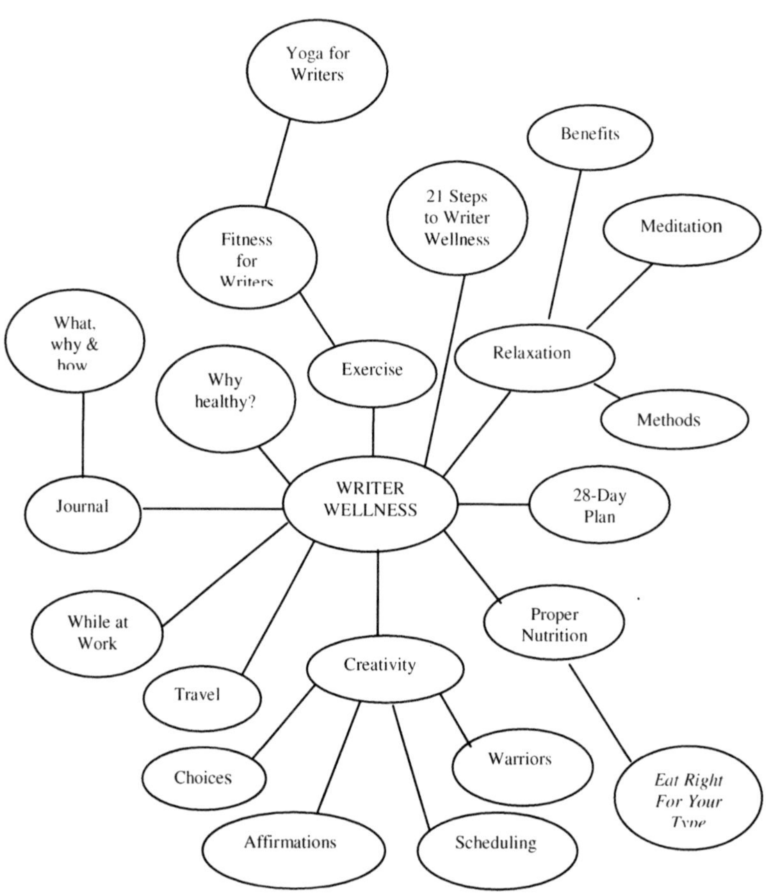

About the author Joy E. Held

Joy is the mother of two teenage daughters. She has home schooled her children for the last ten years.

Joy is a graduate of Glenville State College with a Liberal Arts bachelors degree and she has an associates degree in Early Childhood Education. She is licensed and certified in Kindermusik and is a Registered Yoga Teacher-500.

On the weekends, Joy presents a variety of workshops for adults.

She volunteers at the Actors Guild of Parkersburg as a choreographer.

Currently she teaches dance, hatha yoga, creative writing and early childhood music at the Mid Ohio Valley Ballet Academy of Fine Arts. She is the editor of the studio newsletter.

Writer Wellness is her first nonfiction title. She searches for a publisher for her completed historical novel *Message To Love*, set during the Spanish-American War in Cuba, and has begun writing another romance set against the French and Indian War of 1755.

She is published widely in newspapers, literary magazines, and a variety of arts trade journals including *Dance Teacher Now, Juggler's World, Gambit Journal,* and *Dance Teacher of London*. She is a past member of the board of directors for the Ohio Valley Literary Group. She is a member of West Virginia Writers, Inc., Central Ohio Fiction Writers and Romance Writers of America. Additionally, she is an educational consultant for the Mid Ohio Valley Ballet.

She resides in West Virginia and enjoys journal writing, walking, and reading.

Unleash the creative writer in you!

Writer Wellness

Inspiration, guidance, and
exercises for writers in:

Journaling
Relaxation
Fitness
Nutrition
Creative Play

To schedule a workshop or
speaking engagement contact:

Joy Held
P.O. Box 1322
Parkersburg, WV 26102-1322
E-mail: joybeth@wirefire.com
www.writerwellness.com
or
New Leaf Books at
info@newleafbooks.net

Enjoy the journey!

Expand your horizons

with more great reads from
New Leaf Books

Romance:

- ❑ ***A Find Through Time*** by Marianne Petit 1-930076-18-5 $8.50 ______
- ❑ ***Kyros' Secret*** by Elizabeth Rose 1-930076-03-7 $8.50 ______
- ❑ ***The Oracle of Delphi*** by Elizabeth Rose 1-930076-33-9 $8.50 ______
- ❑ ***Thief of Olympus*** by Elizabeth Rose 1-930076-09-6 $8.50 ______

Mystery/Suspense:

- ❑ ***Valley of Hemlock*** by Eden Reed 1-930076-25-8 $8.50 ______
- ❑ ***Saving Jake*** by Ophelia Julien 1-930076-15-0 $8.50 ______
- ❑ ***Catch a Falling Lawyer*** by Robert Smith 1-930076-11-8 $8.50 ______
- ❑ ***World Under Siege*** by Stanley J. Gulik 1-930076-30-4 $10.50 ______

Sci-Fi/Thriller:

- ❑ ***X'd Out*** by Eric Hermanson 1-930076-05-3 $8.50 ______
- ❑ ***A-list*** by Eric Hermanson 1-930076-07-X $8.50 ______

Nonfiction:

- ❑ ***A Philistine's Journal*** by Wayne Turmel 1-930076-13-4 $8.50 ______
- ❑ ***Lucy's Letters*** by Nancy Langer Schlecht 1-930076-40-1 $11.50 ______
- ❑ ***Writer Wellness*** by Joy E. Held 1-930076-00-2 $11.50 ______

Total ______

Shipping & handling: $2.00 for the first book ($5 for outside US); $1.00 for each additional book. IL residents include 6.75% tax. No cash.

Make check or money order payable in US funds to
WIGWAM PUBLISHING CO.
P.O. Box 6992
Villa Park, IL 60181

Ship to:

Name:______________________________

Address:____________________________

City:__________________State:______Zip:__________

Phone:________________E-mail:______________

Visit us at *www.newleafbooks.net*

Printed in the United States
60865LVS00002B/1-51

9 781930 076006